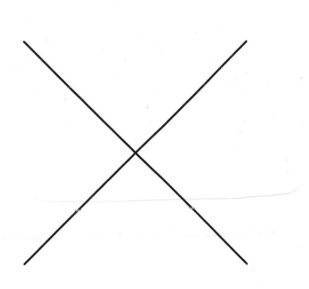

THE END OF WAR

THE END OF WAR

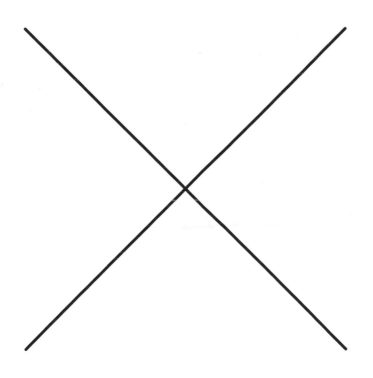

JOHN
HORGAN

McSWEENEY'S BOOKS
SAN FRANCISCO

mcsweeneys.net

Copyright © 2012 John Horgan

Cover design by Brian McMullen

ISBN: 978-1-936365-36-4

Printed in Michigan by Thomson-Shore

For Valerie

CONTENTS

Living in Wartime

I have never served in the military, shot at someone, or been shot at. And yet like everyone else alive today, I have always lived in war's shadow. My grandfather and father were both Navy men. My grandfather, who fought in both World Wars, commanded a troop carrier during the Allied invasions of Salerno and Anzio and was buried in Arlington National Cemetery in 1989. My father attended the Naval Academy and served on a destroyer in World War II. In August 1945, his ship picked up survivors of the *Indianapolis* after it was torpedoed and sunk by a Japanese submarine. Out of 1,196 men on the ship, 880 died, many of them eaten by sharks. Shortly before being sunk, the *Indianapolis* had delivered parts of Little Boy, the bomb that destroyed Hiroshima, to a U.S. air base.

When I was a boy, my father let me play with a Japanese rifle, with the bayonet attached, that he had brought back from the war. The sonic booms of military jets rattled the windows of our house in suburban Connecticut. At my elementary school, teachers instructed my classmates and me to cover our eyes and duck under our desks if we saw a big flash outside. When I graduated from high school, the Vietnam War was raging. I avoided the draft by drawing a high number in the lottery.

Years later I became a science journalist, and I gravitated toward war-related topics. I reported on debates among anthropologists over whether war stems primarily from nature or nurture. I took field trips to the Los Alamos, Lawrence Livermore, and Sandia National Laboratories, where nuclear weapons are designed, and to the Nevada Test Site, a stretch of desert pocked by the craters of hundreds of nuclear detonations. In 1991, after the Persian Gulf War, I traveled to Kuwait to investigate the environmental effects of the oil wells set aflame by Iraqi troops. I toured the "highway of death" north of Kuwait City, where U.S. planes strafed and bombed Iraqis fleeing back to Baghdad. The bodies had been removed, but the shattered Iraqi trucks, tanks, and troops carriers still reeked of rotting flesh. Sometimes the smoke from the oil fires grew so thick I couldn't see my notebook.

Even in Philipstown, the idyllic township in the Hudson Highlands where I have lived since 1990, war intrudes. You can occasionally hear the thunder of mortars and howitzers from the artillery range at the West Point Military Academy, across the river from us. If the wind is blowing in the right direction, the rat-tat-tat of small-arms fire drifts northward from Camp Smith, an Army training base south of Philipstown where troops practice anti-insurgency maneuvers.

On September 11, 2001, I climbed a hill near my home and looked south toward the New York skyline. I could see only smoke where the Twin Towers had once been visible above the horizon. As I made my way back home, my thoughts turned to my kids, Mac (who was eight then) and Skye (who was six). What would I tell them about this terrible event? How would this affect their lives? Peace seemed awfully remote on 9/11, and during the subsequent U.S. invasions of Afghanistan and Iraq. In spite of these setbacks, I have faith that Mac and Skye will live to see a world without war.

MY SURVEYS

Not many people share this faith. I first realized how pessimistic most people are about the prospects for permanent peace in 2003, during the U.S. invasion of Iraq. An Episcopal priest in my hometown, Frank Geer, asked me to speak to his congregation about whether war is "in our genes." I told Frank's parishioners that war seems to be both primordial and perhaps partially innate; chimpanzees, our closest genetic relatives, engage in deadly group raids, and so did prehistoric humans. Some men seem to get a kick out of killing; the *New York Times* had just quoted an Army sharpshooter saying, "We had a great day. We killed a lot of people." Nonetheless I ended with the obligatory upbeat coda: if the capacity for war is in our genes, so is the capacity for peace. We will end war someday, I said. The only question is how, and how soon.

I expected my neighbors to share my hope, just as most shared my dovish politics. But when I asked the sixty or so audience members if they thought humanity would ever abolish war, only a dozen—hesitantly—raised their hands. This was no anomaly. Ever since that evening, I've obsessively asked people whether they think war will end, once and for all. I've carried out polls whenever I have a captive audience—at talks I've given around the U.S. and in Europe, on the internet, at parties, even in the street. Over 80 percent of those I've queried—liberal, conservative, male, female, affluent, poor, educated, uneducated—say that war will never end.

A survey I carried out for the show "RadioLab" was typical. I approached a score of pedestrians on the streets of Hoboken, where I teach, and asked them if humans would ever stop fighting wars. I got three tentative Yeses and seventeen immediate, adamant Nos. "No," replied Mark, a sixty-year-old dentist, "because of greed, and one-upmanship, and the hierarchy of power, in which everybody wants more." War "is a universal law of life," agreed Patel, a twenty-four-year-old computer scientist. "To get something, you have to fight for something."

Young people seem especially fatalistic. I teach a course called "War and Human Nature" at my university. One assignment requires my students to ask ten or more classmates: "Will humans ever stop fighting wars, once and for all? Why or why not?" More than 90 percent of the four hundred or so respondents said "no." The justifications were diverse: "We're naturally evil" was especially common. "People are always going to hate and try to destroy 'inferiors.'" "Monkeys fight with each other and because humans are animals too, we follow that pattern." "Men are power crazy and women are not in power." "People would just get bored with no war."

Even more disconcertingly, some of those who answered "Yes" revealed in their explanations that they were actually pessimists: "Yes, because in the future the human species will unite to fight alien species." "Yes, but it will only happen under the same one religion, because one's beliefs are a driving force." "Yes. When someone (Korea) launches a nuclear weapon. Then we'll all stop messing with each other and keep it cool." "Yes. Humanity will end wars once everyone is killed." So, war will cease after we band together to fight alien invaders, we all convert to the same religion, we undergo a nuclear attack, or we all die.

Many authorities on war share this lack of faith. One of the Hudson Highland's chief cultural attractions is the West Point Museum of the U.S. Military Academy. The museum offers a tour of the entire history of weaponry: Paleolithic stone axes, slings, chariots, crossbows, cannons (which during the Civil War were forged in Philipstown, where I live), blunderbusses, pistols, grenades, mortars, howitzers, machine guns, tanks, and bombers. The tour culminates with a replica of Fat Man, the atomic bomb dropped on Nagasaki in 1945. The displays are weirdly reminiscent of those showing the evolution of life, with increasingly deadly weapons substituted for organisms.

Proclamations throughout the museum heighten the sense of war's inevitability. One, unattributed, reads: "Unquestionably, war-making is an aspect of human nature which will continue as nations attempt to impose their will upon each other." Others quote Churchill: "Nothing is worse than war? Dishonor is worse than war. Slavery is worse than war"; Thucydides: "Peace is an armistice in a war that is continuously going on";

and Plato: "Only the dead have seen the end of war." Actually, the museum got this final attribution wrong. The philosopher George Santayana uttered these words as a bitter rebuke to descriptions of World War I as "the war to end all wars."

The U.S. Commander-in-Chief, President Barack Obama, also seems to lack faith in our ability to overcome war any time soon. On December 1, 2009, I heard a fleet of helicopters thrumming past my home, bearing Obama and his retinue to West Point. There, Obama told an assembly of cadets that, after months of deliberation, he had decided to send thirty thousand more troops to Afghanistan. Nine days later, while accepting the Nobel Peace Prize in Oslo, Norway, Obama declared: "War, in one form or another, appeared with the first man." He added: "We must begin by acknowledging the hard truth: we will not eradicate violent conflict in our lifetimes." Obama seemed to be echoing the message promoted at the West Point Museum: *We have always fought, and we always will.*

SEEING WAR AS A CHOICE

I wrote this book to challenge that gloomy attitude, and to make the case that the end of war is possible, and even imminent. My optimism stems not from wishful thinking—or not *just* from wishful thinking—but from scientific investigations of warfare. Since I preached to my Philipstown neighbors in 2003, I have immersed myself much more deeply in research on war, and as a result I have become much more upbeat about the prospects for permanent peace. What was once a faith based on moral conviction has become a belief based on empirical evidence.

War seems, at first glance, to defy scientific analysis. Scientists have tried, in vain, to trace war to a single cause or set of causes—whether genetic, ecological, economic, political, or cultural. This failure is not surprising, given war's enormous complexity and mutability. Think about it with me for a moment: if war is defined as deadly, organized fighting between two or more groups, that definition includes the feuding of Yanomamö hunters in Amazonia, the clash of competing chiefdoms on Easter Island, Alexander's conquest of Persia, the Crusades, the Napoleonic wars, World Wars I and II, the civil conflicts rending Colombia and Sudan, and a thousand other skirmishes and full-on battles. Consider the differences in combatants, weaponry, tactics, politics, purported causes, and cultural contexts just in wars involving Americans: from the War of Independence to the Indian Wars, the Civil War, the Spanish-American War, the Korean War, the Vietnam War, the first and second wars against Iraq, the war in Afghanistan, the air war against Libya...

But investigations into war do yield a few compelling insights. First, contrary to what I suggested to my neighbors in 2003, war is not innate. Let me say that again: we are not hardwired for war. Evidence of lethal group violence dates back *not* to the emergence of the *Homo* genus millions of years ago, nor to the emergence of our species hundreds of thousands of years ago, but to less than thirteen thousand years ago, shortly before the dawn of civilization. Moreover, from prehistory up through the present, many societies have resisted the allure of war and militarism, belying the notion of a biological drive or an instinct that impels us to fight. In fact, odd as it may sound, humanity as a whole has recently turned away from war, at least by some yardsticks. Annual war-related casualties have dropped more than ten-fold since the cataclysmic first half of the twentieth century—even as the world's population has surged.

The most important lesson to emerge from research on lethal conflict is both subtle and profound: war is not something that happens to us. We make it happen. In other words, war is not foisted on us by forces beyond our control, whether innate male aggression, competition for scarce resources, or entrenched cultural attitudes. Wars all begin with human decisions. Choices. Of course, throughout history some people—chiefs, pharaohs, kings, emperors, autocrats, presidents, and warlords—have had the power to impose their choices (for good or ill) on others. But a crucial reason for the decline in war over the past half century is the worldwide surge in democracy since the end of World War II. Democracy does not guarantee peace. In fact, the desire for freedom can result in conflict. But more people are living more freely today than at any time in history, and they are choosing peace over war.

Forecasting human affairs is a tricky, paradoxical business. Isaac Asimov made this point in his great science-fiction series *Foundation*. A central character is the brilliant mathematician Hari Seldon, who creates a computer model that predicts the future of societies, just as statistical mechanics predicts the behavior of gases. The model is limited in one crucial way: if people learn about their destiny, they may avoid it by changing their behavior. Seldon's model predicts the collapse of the galactic empire into a catastrophic civil war, but he never makes his prophecy public, and so it comes true.

If Seldon had revealed his forecast, war might have broken out anyway; factions within the empire might have launched preemptive strikes against each other instead of pursuing peace. Human choice—free will—is the wild card, the asterisk that must be appended to all predictions about humanity. So I am not offering a prediction here so much as a prescription: we can end war if we want and choose to end it.

NOT EVEN WRONG

Scholars often squabble over war's definition. Should the term include chimpanzee assaults? Feuds among hunter-gatherers? State-sponsored genocide, like the Nazi slaughter of Jews? Or just conflicts between uniformed soldiers? In this book I use the term broadly to describe lethal group violence of all kinds. I do not want to be accused, as some scholars are, of minimizing the problem of war in our evolutionary past—or in the present, for that matter—by defining the term too narrowly. When I talk about the end of war, however, I mean first and foremost war (and even the threat of war) between nations. I envision military clashes between any two nations becoming as inconceivable as war is now between Germany and France, the U.S. and Canada, even New York and New Jersey. My hope, and expectation, is that other forms of large-scale violence—genocide, civil wars, insurgencies, terrorist attacks, and killings by criminal gangs—will eventually become rare as well.

I believe war will end for scientific reasons; I believe war *must* end for moral reasons. War has always struck me as not only wrong but crazy, absurd, contradictory—even when fought for seemingly noble reasons. The cognitive dissonance that war generates in me has grown over the years, and it stems in part from my growing affection and admiration for my species, in spite of all its flaws. Our remarkable progress—scientific, technological, medical, political, moral—makes war's persistence all the more unfathomable.

Even in war zones, combatants routinely carry out acts of heroic kindness and generosity toward each other. Soldiers and government officials often complain that journalists fail to report positive news, but feel-good stories are staples of war journalism. Take, for example, an article published in the *New York Times* in 2010. The reporter, C.J. Chivers, describes how a U.S. Black Hawk helicopter crew flew an Afghan woman enduring a prolonged, painful labor to a Red Cross hospital, where doctors helped her deliver a healthy boy. The story is straight, unsentimental reporting—Chivers notes that the helicopter crew only undertook the mission after ensuring that no nearby American or Afghan units needed assistance—but moving nonetheless.

But consider these incidents involving U.S. soldiers in Afghanistan in 2010: in February, American and Afghan special forces stormed a home in southeastern Afghanistan, shooting to death two Afghan men and three women, two of whom were pregnant. The soldiers initially claimed that the women were already dead of knife wounds when they entered the house, but Afghan investigators claimed that the soldiers had dug bullets out of the women's bodies to cover up the shooting. Although they denied the cover-up, U.S. military officials eventually accepted responsibility for the women's deaths.

That same month, U.S. drone operators in Nevada reported spotting armed Afghans traveling in three trucks in Oruzgan province. A helicopter fired missiles at the vehicles, which turned out to be carrying not militants but civilians, including women and children. The attack killed twenty-three people and wounded twelve others. The U.S. commander in Afghanistan, General Stanley McCrystal, apologized for the "mistake."

While reading about these sickening events in the *New York Times*, I was also following the trial of Steven Hayes, who together with an accomplice, broke into a home in Connecticut belonging to a husband and wife and their two daughters. After ransacking the house, the men raped and strangled the wife, raped one daughter and then doused her and her sister with gasoline and set them on fire. The men savagely beat the father, but he alone survived. After a protracted, expensive trial, a jury convicted Hayes, and the judge sentenced him to death, more than three years after his crime.

It struck me, reading about the trial, that my country treats a rapist-murderer with more judicious, careful thought than innocent civilians in a foreign war zone. This contrast encapsulates war's insanity. Even when civilians are spared, even when soldiers fight justly for a just cause, like the defeat of fascism, war demeans us. The physicist Wolfgang Pauli liked to disparage truly bad theories as "not even wrong." That is an apt description for war. Even when it's seemingly "just" or "right," war is so wrong that it is not even wrong.

In the end, no matter what science reveals about war's roots, I think we are morally bound to seek its end or reduction, just as we must try to abolish rape and racism in spite of any alleged genetic underpinnings for these behaviors. Even the most hawk-ish fatalists acknowledge as much. So let's say researchers con-firm that our ancestors waged war for millions of years, and that natural selection favored genes that predispose some males to enjoy chopping people into little bits. These findings, however daunting they would be, would not let us off the hook. But sci-ence fortunately reveals that war, far from being deeply rooted in our nature, is a recent human invention that many societies have relinquished. We have no good excuses to keep fighting.

ENDING WAR VERSUS CURING CANCER

Optimists have proclaimed the imminence of peace many times in the past. In 1848, John Stuart Mill suggested that com-merce between nations was "rapidly rendering war obsolete, by strengthening and multiplying the personal interests which act in opposition to it." The British journalist and politician Norman Angell offered similar arguments in 1909 in his inter-national best seller *The Great Illusion*, which asserted that the nations of Europe no longer had any rational reason to fight.

Never mind that World War I actually bore out Angell's claim that war's destructive consequences vastly outweigh its benefits, even for victors. Past prophecies of world peace raise a legitimate question: if a predicted event keeps failing to occur, at what point should we stop believing the predic-tion? It depends on what's being predicted. The chemist Linus Pauling, the only person to win two unshared Nobel Prizes, devoted himself to ending both war and cancer. He won a Nobel Prize in chemistry in 1954 for explaining the chemical bond in quantum terms. In 1962 he won the Nobel Peace Prize for helping to bring about a U.S.–Soviet ban on atmospheric nuclear testing. Pauling spent the final decades of his life seeking ways to prevent and cure cancer.

In his 1958 book *No More War!* Pauling wrote: "We are living through that unique epoch in the history of civilization when war will cease to be the means of settling great world problems." He urged the U.N. to form a "World Peace Research Organization" dedicated to solving "problems of the kind that have in the past led to war." Twenty-five years later, in the preface to the 1983 edition of *No More War!*, Pauling expressed hope that after another twenty-five years "there will be no need to republish the book, because the goal of world peace will have been achieved, militarism and nuclear weapons will have been brought under control, and the threat of world destruction will finally have been abolished."

2008 has come and gone, and we still live in the shadow of war and militarism. Cancer also continues to ravage humanity, in spite of the efforts of Pauling (felled by prostate cancer in 1994) and many others. Given the poor record of cancer research, we should certainly be skeptical when scientists say a cure is imminent, as they have countless times over the past few decades. But we don't mock them or tell them to abandon their search just because they have failed so far. Cancer is such a scourge that we could never—nor should we—cease trying to overcome it.

Like cancer, war causes immense suffering, and it diverts vast amounts of human energy, intelligence, and resources away from other dire problems. But war and cancer differ in one crucial way: whereas cancer is something that happens to us, war is entirely our creation. This sets war apart not only from diseases like cancer but also from droughts, storms, floods, earthquakes, and tsunamis. Yes, we can stop smoking to curb cancer rates. We can reduce our consumption of fossil fuels to make droughts, floods, and hurricanes less likely. We can construct buildings and early-warning systems to minimize the devastation from earthquakes and tsunamis. But for the foreseeable future, these natural disasters will continue to afflict us. War, on the other hand, could end tomorrow through a simple act of will on the part of a relatively small number of leaders and combatants around the world.

Pessimists—who sometimes call themselves realists—dismiss world peace as a utopian or even religious fantasy. But the end of war does not mean the end of all conflict, as skeptics often imply. If large-scale military violence ceases, the world will still be roiled by economic, political, ethnic, and religious disputes. Most people will simply find ways to resolve differences without killing each other by the dozens, hundreds, thousands, or millions.

STAYING UPBEAT

One of my classrooms offers a magnificent view of the Hudson River and the Manhattan skyline. This perspective comes in handy when I talk to my students about war. When they tell me that people will fight as long as some have more stuff than others, or as long as people hold different political and religious views, I point across the river at the skyscrapers of New York and say: that disproves what you are saying. New Yorkers include people of every possible race, ethnic background, and creed, poor people and rich, Muslims, Christians, Jews, Hindus, and atheists, right-wing Republicans, and hard-core lefties. New Yorkers bicker incessantly about many things, but with rare exceptions they do not settle disputes by bombing or machine-gunning each other.

I have moments—days—of doubt. One began when I asked students in my "War and Human Nature" course if they had been in a physical fight within the previous five years. I wanted to make the point that violence is rare, but to my dismay virtually all of the students—including several women!—raised their hands. When I walked into my house that evening, I found my son Mac in the living room gleefully assembling an "Airsoft" sniper rifle—an electric-powered BB gun modeled after the M-4 used by many U.S. troops—that had just arrived in the mail. Mac participates in Airsoft war games with scores of other camouflaged enthusiasts, many of them veterans of real combat in Iraq and Afghanistan. He also eagerly consumes documentaries and books about war. Once, when I expressed puzzlement over his fascination with war, Mac reminded me that my grandfather and father were soldiers; I, the peacenik, am the oddball.

When my faith in a warless future wavers, I remind myself that in the late 1980s humanity still faced the threat of a global nuclear holocaust that could destroy not just the U.S. and U.S.S.R., but all life on Earth. Then, incredibly, the Soviet Union dissolved and the cold war ended peacefully. Apartheid ended in South Africa without significant violence, and democracy has spread elsewhere as well. President Obama and the president of Russia have begun slashing their nuclear arsenals, and Obama is carrying out his campaign promise to pull American troops out of Iraq. Early in 2011, unarmed protesters in Tunisia and Egypt toppled two corrupt, repressive regimes, inspiring similar protests throughout the Islamic world. Yes, some of these protests provoked violent counter-reactions. But humanity, in starts and fits, still seems to be headed toward a world with less and less war.

To keep my mood upbeat, I pin anti-war slogans to the bulletin board facing my desk. One is a sticker from the Fellowship of Reconciliation, a venerable anti-war group, which reads: "There is no way to peace. Peace is the way." Beside that is a full-page ad that Yoko Ono placed in the *New York Times* on the fortieth anniversary of its original publication as a protest against the Vietnam War. The ad proclaims in huge type WAR IS OVER, and adds in small letters at the bottom of the page, "if you want it." Wishful thinking, perhaps, but also—I hope to persuade you—scientifically supportable statements.

If you find this book totally persuasive, I'd be thrilled. But my more realistic goal is to start a conversation about why we fight and how we can stop. I invite you pessimists, especially, to question your attitudes toward war. I hope to provoke you into talking to others about their views on these questions. If you're unimpressed by the diagnoses and prescriptions offered in this book, come up with new ones! If we all want peace—and every sane person does—surely we're smart enough to achieve it. Or rather, choose it. When we start believing that we can end war, we're already well on our way.

CHAPTER ONE

War Is Not Innate

To get my students to appreciate war's knotty contradictions, I ask them to propose causes of war, which I then scrawl on the whiteboard. They typically nominate these candidates: innate male aggression, ambition, greed, the desire for freedom, religion, ethnic differences, capitalism, patriotism, overpopulation, poverty, inequality, the military–industrial complex, the media, stupidity, and boredom.

This exercise helps me make a few crucial points. First, war has no single cause, not even close. Nor does it have a single solution. And some factors that trigger conflict can also help suppress it. In other words, they are both causes and solutions. Religion, for example, has certainly motivated many warriors, from bloodthirsty Christian crusaders in the Middle Ages to the al Qaeda terrorists who attacked the U.S. on September 11, 2001. But religion has inspired many pacifist sects, such as the Quakers and Jains, as well as leaders of nonviolent social change like Gandhi and Martin Luther King (who, it seems worthwhile to note, were both aggressive, ambitious men). As for nationalism, some thinkers, notably Jean-Jacques Rousseau, saw the state as a cause of bloodshed, while others, such as Thomas Hobbes, viewed it as the cure. Marx blamed war on capitalism, but some modern economists see capitalism as our best hope for reducing poverty, and by extension social unrest.

Science represents another problem that is also a solution. Science contributes to conflict, even as it fortifies my optimism that war can end. Scientists help to produce new-and-improved methods for humans to destroy each other, from catapults and cannons to nuclear submarines and drones. Innovations in weaponry spur arms races that destabilize relations between nations, and often culminate in war (although some nuclear enthusiasts insist that without the deterrent effect of hydrogen bombs, the cold war would surely have become white hot).

Scientific theories can also mutate into divisive, deadly ideologies. Marx hoped his economic system would help humanity achieve a just, peaceful utopia; instead, communism inspired countless bloody insurgencies, one of which, in Russia, spawned a horrendously brutal, totalitarian regime. Similarly, the writings of Darwin and other nineteenth-century biologists yielded social Darwinism and eugenics, which culminated in Nazism. In the twentieth century, as I point out to my religion-averse students, secular and pseudo-scientific ideologies killed far more people than religion did. What makes a belief system lethal, I suggest, is its adherents' conviction that it is absolutely true, so much so that they feel justified in eliminating non-believers.

Science also exacerbates the problem of war in more subtle ways by, for instance, emphasizing genetic contributions to human behavior and downplaying cultural factors. Of course, all organisms are products of genes as well as their environment and experiences, all of which interact in complex ways. The question remains: how much does nature contribute to a given behavior? The more deeply a behavior is rooted in our biology, the less choice we may have to change. Is war a choice, or are we hardwired for it?

AGAINST GENETIC DETERMINISM

After World War II, the debate over whether we are products primarily of nature or nurture tipped temporarily toward nurture. The Nazis had given biological ideas about human nature a bad name. But since the 1970s, researchers in sociobiology, evolutionary psychology, and behavioral genetics have become increasingly insistent that our genes—more than our upbringing, education, and culture—shape our behavior, including our tendency to fight wars. Other scientists objected to this trend on political as well as scientific grounds, arguing that biological explanations of war would discourage attempts to abolish it.

In the 1980s, David Adams, a psychologist at Wesleyan University, sought to document the ill effects of biological theories of war. Adams and a colleague asked 126 students at Wesleyan and other schools whether they thought "wars are inevitable because human beings are naturally aggressive." Thirty-three percent of the respondents said "yes" to that statement, and 40 percent agreed with the statement that "war is intrinsic to human nature." Students with these views were less likely to work for disarmament and peace. Surveys carried out in Finland during the same period produced similar results.

Adams was horrified at how many young people felt humanity was doomed to wage war. "These results," he writes, "support the need for a worldwide educational campaign to dispel the myth that war is instinctive, intrinsic to human nature, or unavoidable because of an alleged biological basis." In 1986, he and nineteen other scientists—including specialists in neuroscience, genetics, and other fields—sought to launch such a campaign. Meeting in Seville, Spain, under the auspices of the United Nations, the scientists drafted a statement that begins with five propositions:

1. It is scientifically incorrect to say that we have inherited a tendency to make war from our animal ancestors.

2. It is scientifically incorrect to say that war or any other violent behavior is genetically programmed into our human nature.

3. It is scientifically incorrect to say that in the course of human evolution there has been a selection for aggressive behavior more than for other kinds of behavior.

4. It is scientifically incorrect to say that humans have a "violent brain."

5. It is scientifically incorrect to say that war is caused by "instinct" or any single motivation.

The statement concludes "that biology does not condemn humanity to war, and that humanity can be freed from the bondage of biological pessimism... The same species who invented war is capable of inventing peace. The responsibility lies with each of us." UNESCO, the United Nations Educational, Scientific and Cultural Organization, approved the Seville Statement in 1989, and has disseminated it ever since. The statement has been endorsed by dozens of educational, political, and scientific organizations, including the American Anthropological Association and the American Psychological Association.

The Seville Statement is an accurate reflection of research on warfare and other forms of violence. Since Adams carried out his poll in the mid-1980s, though, people young and old have become more pessimistic, if my surveys are any guide. One reason may be that many scientists—including some who share the anti-war sentiments of Adams—dismiss the Seville Statement as an inappropriate or quixotic attempt to impose a political agenda on science. A more important factor, I suspect, is the widespread acceptance of a dramatic theory of the origins of warfare, based primarily on observations not of humans, but of chimpanzees.

THE MYTH OF THE DEMONIC MALE

As recently as the early 1970s, most scientists considered humans to be the only primates that kill each other on a regular basis. This assumption was challenged by an event that took place at the Gombe Reserve in Tanzania, where Jane Goodall had been observing chimpanzees since 1960. Chimps, whose formal name is *Pan troglodytes*, typically form communities with as many as several hundred members. In 1974, a researcher at Gombe named Hillali Matama watched a band of seven male chimpanzees and a female from one community attack and kill a young male, whom Goodall had named Godi, from a neighboring group.

What made this case remarkable was not simply its violence. Although sometimes Goodall emphasized the sweetness of *Pan troglodytes* in her early writings, she and her colleagues had witnessed chimps, especially alpha males, biting and beating others within their group, sometimes viciously. But Godi's death resulted from an attack of members of one chimpanzee community on a member of another community, which was unprecedented. Other researchers subsequently observed similar inter-group raids at Gombe and elsewhere.

What makes these episodes especially disturbing is that *Homo sapiens* is more closely related to *Pan troglodytes* than to any other species, and vice versa. Genetic analyses reveal that our lineages diverged less than 7 million years ago, and we still share 98 percent of each other's genes. Chimpanzee genes overlap more with our genes than they do with those of gorillas, orangutans, or other apes (with the notable exception of bonobos, whom I will discuss shortly).

A British-born anthropologist, Richard Wrangham, was doing field research at Gombe at the time of the attack on Godi in 1974. The incident had a profound impact on him, and he has spent much of his career studying what he calls "coalitionary killing" among chimpanzees. His 1996 book *Demonic Males*, co-written with the journalist Dale Peterson, opens with

Wrangham's recollection of how explosive conflict between the Tutsis and Hutus, which eventually killed almost 1 million Rwandans, thwarted his attempt to do field research in an African rain forest. Wrangham draws an analogy between this horrific inter-group violence and that of chimpanzees. "Chimpanzee-like violence," he writes, "preceded and paved the way for human war, making modern humans the dazed survivors of a continuous, 5-million-year habit of lethal aggression."

Wrangham contends that this "habit" is innate, because throughout our evolutionary history, natural selection has favored males with a predisposition not just for aggression, but for lethal group violence. His most disturbing claim is that both male chimpanzees and male humans engage in group attacks not for any particular purpose—such as gaining mates or territory—but because they like it. Human males "enjoy the opportunity to go and beat up on the neighbors," he says, as long as they have little risk of being beaten themselves. Wrangham calls human males "natural warriors."

Wrangham is a charming, genial man. Far from being a warmonger, he is a dove who marched in protests against the U.S. invasion of Iraq in 2003. But he seems to take pleasure in rubbing peoples' faces in the supposed ferocity of our species' closest relatives. In 2009, while lecturing at a conference in Salt Lake City on the evolution of aggression, Wrangham showed a film in which five screaming chimpanzees savagely beat a member of a neighboring group. When the victim went limp, Wrangham threw his arms up, like a football referee signaling a touchdown, and yelled, "Yay, our side won!"

When I ask Wrangham if he thinks war will ever end, he

pauses before answering. "I'm not so fatalistic that I'd say we can never do it," he finally replies, "but I would just not want to minimize the obstacles." Wishful thinking about peace, he suggests, can propagate war. If Bush officials had shared his perspective, he contends, they would never have invaded Iraq in 2003, because they would have realized that the attack would probably result in violence and anarchy rather than peace and democracy. "It was so predictable!" he exclaims.

Our best hope for creating a peaceful world, Wrangham suggests, is for women to gain more political power. "My little dream," he tells me, is that all nations give equal decision-making power to two entities, which he called "a House of Men and a House of Women." On the other hand, in *Demonic Males*, Wrangham blames males' aggressive behavior in part on females' sexual preferences. "In the real world," he writes, "the tough guy finds himself besieged with female admirers, while the self-effacing friend sadly clutches his glass of Chablis at the fern bar alone."

One might think that most people would dismiss the behavior of apes as irrelevant to debates about human war. But *Demonic Males* has impressed many readers, including some in positions of power. Hillary Clinton is reportedly a fan of the book. So is the political philosopher Francis Fukuyama, who served in the State Department under President George H.W. Bush and wrote *The End of History* and other widely discussed books. Whereas Wrangham suggests empowering women as a solution to war, Fukuyama sees it as a potential problem. In an article in the journal *Foreign Affairs*, Fukuyama expresses concern that "feminine" political leaders like Norway's Gro BrundHand might not be tough enough to deal with demonic males like Saddam Hussein.

Wrangham's theory has also been cited favorably by a host of recent books, including *Sex and War* by the physician Malcolm Potts and journalist Thomas Hayden, *The Most Dangerous Animal* by the philosopher David Livingstone Smith, and *The Blank Slate* by the Harvard psychologist Steven Pinker. Pinker is one of the most respected modern proponents of gene-centric theories of human behavior. "Chimpicide," he writes, "raises the possibility that the forces of evolution, not just the idiosyncrasies of a particular culture, prepared us for violence."

DEBUNKING THE MYTH

"Extraordinary claims," the astronomer Carl Sagan liked to say, "require extraordinary evidence." Wrangham's assertion that lethal group violence dates back millions of years to our common ancestor with chimpanzees qualifies as an extraordinary claim, with profound significance for human affairs. But Wrangham's evidence, far from extraordinary, is weak. Wrangham never adequately establishes that chimpanzees, let *al*one humans, are innately predisposed toward war.

Wrangham often presents the rate of coalitionary killing in terms of annual deaths per 100,000. In a 2004 paper, he estimates that "the median death rate from intergroup aggression among chimpanzees is 140 per 100,000, which rises to 356 per 100,000" if suspected cases are included. Wrangham contends that these death rates "are similar to those resulting from war among humans in traditional subsistence societies." (The U.S. homicide rate in 2010, in contrast, was less than six per 100,000 people.)

Based on Wrangham's statistics, one might conclude that researchers have witnessed hundreds or at least scores of coalitionary killings. In fact, as of 2004, researchers had directly witnessed only twelve deaths from lethal intergroup aggression. They "suspected"—based on the discovery of a mutilated corpse or other circumstantial evidence—another seventeen coalitionary killings. These observations are based on 215 total researcher-years of observations of chimpanzee communities at nine separate sites in Africa. That means a researcher watching a typical chimpanzee community will observe, directly or indirectly, only one group killing every seven years. The anthropologist Robert Sussman, who together with his colleague Joshua Marshack compiled these statistics, accuses Wrangham of adopting the "five o'clock news" approach to primate studies: "If it bleeds, it leads." Wrangham's relentless focus on violence, Sussman says, results in a distorted picture of chimps and humans.

Responding to Sussman's critique, Wrangham concedes that chimpanzee coalitionary killings are "certainly rare." He also acknowledges that "there are various sites where scientists have studied chimpanzees without any record of coalitionary killing or other kinds of violence." He suggests that these nonviolent chimpanzees are not "habituated" to their human observers, or are isolated from other chimpanzee communities. But this response raises another question: could unusual environmental conditions be triggering inter-group chimpanzee violence, rather than a "natural" warrior instinct?

Recall that the first deadly gang attack was not witnessed until 1974, after Jane Goodall and others had spent more than a decade closely observing chimpanzees. Nor had previous primatologists—such as the legendary Robert Yerkes, who pioneered observations of chimpanzees in the early twentieth century and even lived with them in his home—witnessed any killings. Goodall, who began supplying bananas to chimpanzees in 1965, expressed concern that the food "was having a marked effect on the behavior of the chimps. They were beginning to move about in large groups more often than they had ever done in the old days. Worst of all, the adult males were becoming increasingly aggressive."

Ian Tattersall, an anthropologist at the American Museum of Natural History, suggests that lethal chimpanzee violence may also be "related to population stress occasioned by human encroachment." Over the past few decades, Africa's human population has surged, and farmers, loggers, and poachers have invaded the habitats of chimpanzees, who can no longer roam freely in search of food.

These environmental factors seem to have altered the cultural behavior of certain chimpanzee communities, leading them to engage in lethal raids on others and even to attack humans. In a paper written with several colleagues, Wrangham himself has emphasized that chimpanzees display "significant cultural variation" in tool use, grooming, courtship, food preparation, and other behaviors. Why, then, does Wrangham insist that coalitionary killing—which even he calls "rare"—stems primarily from males' innate urges?

To explain why coalitionary violence breaks out in certain times and places and not others, Wrangham proposes that male chimpanzees from one group attack outsiders whenever they have a clear advantage. The same is true of human males, Wrangham asserts. One obvious objection to this thesis is that many powerful societies refrain from attacking weaker ones. The U.S. could easily crush Canada but somehow restrains itself. Why? When I put this question to Wrangham, he replies that "there must also be a state of hostility between the two meeting groups." But this explanation is circular. The question is: what caused the hostility in the first place?

Wrangham concedes that his imbalance-of-power hypothesis cannot explain the "enormous variation in the rates of intergroup killing among human societies." When it comes to modern nations in particular, "the roles of specialized military units, hierarchical leadership, huge groups, diverse weaponry, elaborate alliance systems, and other features specific to state organization are significant complicating factors." More simply put, culture matters—precisely the point made by Wrangham's critics.

FRANS DE WAAL AND THE HIPPIE CHIMPS

To get a more rounded picture of chimpanzees and other primates, I visited Frans de Waal at the Yerkes Primate Research Center in Georgia, which houses chimpanzees and monkeys. We spoke in a watchtower overlooking a fenced-in compound where three male chimpanzees and a dozen females lolled, lazily nitpicking or sniffing each other. While not denying that chimpanzees can be violent—he has witnessed gruesome attacks himself—de Waal says that Wrangham has created a cartoonishly distorted picture of the species.

Over decades of observing chimpanzees, de Waal collected overwhelming evidence of chimpanzees' generosity, empathy, and peace-making. Chimps often hug and kiss each other and share food both to avoid fights and to make up after them. If one chimp has been injured, others will console it by licking its wounds. Chimpanzees are capable of extraordinary altruism toward members of their communities. They cannot swim, and hence they can easily panic and drown, even in shallow water. Because chimps fear water, zoos often surround chimpanzee compounds with moats. Yet male and female chimpanzees have died after plunging into moats to rescue others who have fallen into the water.

De Waal acknowledges that the most common species of chimpanzee, *Pan troglodytes*, does not treat members of outside communities so kindly, but bonobos do. Discovered in the forests of the Congo in 1929, bonobos were initially viewed as a subspecies of chimpanzee before being classified as a separate type altogether, *Pan paniscus*. Genetic analyses suggest that the two chimp species diverged 1 or 2 million years ago. Sometimes called pygmy chimps, bonobos are darker-skinned and more slender than *Pan troglodytes*, but are otherwise about the same size. (The descriptors "paniscus," which means diminutive, and "pygmy" are really misnomers.)

Only in the past few decades has the bonobos' extraordinary social behavior come to light. Male bonobos do not dominate their communities as male *Pan troglodytes* do. Although male bonobos occasionally beat and bite each other, they are much less violent than *Pan troglodytes* males. Researchers have not witnessed a single killing either within or between bonobo communities. Even more remarkably, bonobos engage in homosexual as well as heterosexual acts, including mutual masturbation, oral sex, and tongue kissing. Males and females often copulate face-to-face, missionary style, which chimpanzees do only rarely. "The frontal orientation of the bonobo vulva and clitoris strongly suggest that the female genitalia are adapted for this position," de Waal says.

Sex smoothes relations between as well as within communities. When bonobos from different groups meet, "females often rush to the other side to have sex with both males and other females," de Waal writes. "Since it is hard to have sex and wage war at the same time, the scene rapidly turns into a sort of picnic." This promiscuity reduces violence between bonobo communities just as intermarriage does between human tribes, de Waal suspects. Bonobos display empathy and altruism even toward other species. In one case, an adult male rescued a duckling being harassed by two young bonobos and released it back into its moat.

Some critics charge that the reputation of the "Hippie Chimps"—for making love, not war—has been overblown. Researchers recently observed bonobos killing monkeys for food, as *Pan troglodytes* does. But de Waal and others have repeatedly confirmed bonobos' relatively benign behavior toward each other in captivity and the wild. Bonobos are just as closely related to us as their chimpanzee cousins, de Waal notes, and hence "exactly, equally relevant to this whole discussion about the origins of warfare."

In fact, de Waal contends, there are good reasons to believe that bonobos are "more representative of our primate background" than *Pan troglodytes*. As evidence, he cites recent studies of the extinct primate species *Ardipithecus ramidus*, which roamed Ethiopia 4.4 million years ago and is the oldest known human ancestor. Anthropologists discovered the first partial skeleton of "Ardi" in Ethiopia in the early 1990s, and over the next decade they uncovered the remains of nine more individuals, all over 4 million years old. Researchers initially classified *Ardipithecus* as a member of the genus *Australopithecus* before deciding that it deserved its own genus.

Ardi "falsifies" the claim that the behavior of our ancestors strongly resembled that of chimpanzees, the anthropologist Owen Lovejoy of Kent State University asserts in a paper published in the prestigious journal *Science* in 2009. *Ardipithecus ramidus* "reveals that the early" hominid evolutionary trajectory differed profoundly from those of our ape relatives." Ardi has triggered a "tectonic shift" in views of human evolution, Lovejoy tells me in an interview. "We now know, especially in light of *Ardipithecus*, that hominids have always been far less aggressive" than chimpanzees.

Ardi's brain was roughly the same size as a chimpanzee's, but in other ways the species was quite different. Ardi's physiology suggests that it could move easily through trees, like chimpanzees, but that it was better adapted for bipedality, or upright walking. Male and female Ardis were closer in size than male and female chimpanzees and so were presumably more likely to engage in pair-bonding. Most importantly, *Ardipithecus* lacked the dagger-like canines that chimpanzees and even bonobos (whose canines are smaller) employ as weapons. These traits persisted in later hominid species such as *Australopithecus*.

As recently as the 1960s, Australopithecenes, which inhabited southern and eastern Africa from 4 to 2 million years ago, were thought to be "killer apes" who hunted each other as well as other animals. This belief was based on the claim of the anthropologist Raymond Dart that cut marks on Australopithecene bones and holes in their skulls were evidence of within-species violence. Popularizations of Dart's work may have inspired the famous "Dawn of Man" scene at the beginning of Stanley Kubrick's 1968 film *2001: A Space Odyssey*, in which one ape-man beats another to death with a bone. The killer ape theory was discredited after other researchers concluded that predators such as leopards caused the bone marks studied by Dart.

SAPOLSKY'S BABOONS

To my mind, the most significant meta-lesson to emerge from research on non-human primates is how malleable, or "plastic" (to use a trendy scientific buzzword), their behavior is. The idea that primate violence stems primarily from hardwired biological impulses reflects "an old way of thinking," de Waal says, "that I don't think fits the facts." De Waal has demonstrated that shifts in environmental conditions can dramatically reduce primate aggression. For example, he has shown that chimpanzees become much less aggressive toward each other if placed in situations in which cooperation will help them obtain more food.

In another experiment, de Waal placed captive adolescent rhesus and stump-tailed macaques together to see how their behavior might change. Although the two species of monkey are genetically almost identical, their behavior is as different as that

of chimps and bonobos. Rhesuses normally dwell in rigid hier-
archies, in which dominant males grab most of the food, enforce
their rule viciously, and rarely reconcile after fights. Stump-tails,
in contrast, are much less aggressive, more egalitarian, and more
likely to make up after fighting with lip-smacking, grooming,
and other behaviors. Within a few months after rhesus and
stump-tails of both sexes lived in captivity together, the rhesuses
were behaving less aggressively and were reconciling after fights
as often as stump-tails.

A still more striking example of primate malleability comes
from an improbable source: baboons, who even more than rhesus monkeys and chimpanzees seem hardwired for aggression.
The evolutionary biologist Edward O. Wilson once said that
if baboons acquired nuclear weapons, "they would destroy the
world in a week." Troops, which include as many as one hundred members, are ruled by alpha males, who typically achieve
high status by beating rivals into submission and thereafter
hog food for themselves. Most males die as a result of fighting.

But even baboons, who seem incorrigibly nasty, can change.
Since the early 1980s, the biologist Robert Sapolsky has traveled to Kenya to spy on a group of baboons that he calls "Forest
Troop." After a tourist lodge started dumping large amounts of
food at a site near the habitat of Forest Troop, some members
began foraging for food at the dump. Because they had to fight
baboons from another troop camped even closer to the dump,
only the toughest males of Forest Troop frequented the dump.

In the mid-1980s, all these males died after contract-
ing tuberculosis from contaminated meat at the dump. The
epidemic initially left Forest Troop with about twice as many

females as males, who were less pugnacious than those who had died. Conflict within the troop dropped dramatically; Sapolsky even observed males grooming each other, which he calls "nearly as unprecedented as baboons sprouting wings." Most remarkable of all, this cultural sea change persisted for more than two decades, even after Forest Troop absorbed males from other nearby populations. "Forest Troop's low aggression/high affiliation society constitutes nothing less than a multigenerational benign culture," Sapolsky writes.

The research of Sapolsky, de Waal, and even Wrangham reveals that the aggressive behavior of our primate cousins, far from being hardwired, is surprisingly flexible and varied. Nurture matters. Yes, chimps, especially males, are prone to violent aggression, but "coalitionary killing" is rare, and seems to be a response to environmental and cultural conditions as much as it is biological. And that's the point: it's not clear-cut. You might even say that chimpanzees have choices, more than they are often given credit for. The plasticity of primate behavior also undercuts a crucial premise of the demonic male theory, which assumes that if chimps have been violent for the past few decades, their ancestors must have always been violent, too. We can't be sure how chimps were behaving a century ago, let *al*one millions of years ago.

THE FIERCE YANOMAMÖ

Of course—I can hear critics saying—just because chimpanzee warfare is not innate doesn't mean, necessarily, that human warfare isn't. Our lineage, after all, diverged from that of chimpanzees and bonobos millions of years ago. That's more than enough time for our ancestors to have acquired a genetic propensity for coalitionary killing. Just in the last million years, humans acquired the capacity for language, which most scientists now claim is programmed into our genes. So the question remains: is war in our genes? Could the Seville Statement apply to chimps and bonobos, but not to humans?

Many people have concluded as much, based in part on fieldwork by the anthropologist Napoleon Chagnon. In 1964, when he was a twenty-six-year-old graduate student, Chagnon trekked deep into the rain forests of the Amazon to study the Yanomamö, a polygynous, tribal people who obtain their food by hunting, gathering, and cultivating small gardens. The Yanomamö live in enclosed villages sheltering as many as three hundred people.

Chagnon hoped the Yanomamö, one of the few isolated indigenous people left in the world, would yield clues to human evolution. His 1968 account of his work, *Yanomamö: The Fierce People*, became one of the best-selling ethnographies ever. Early on, he recalls his first encounter with the Yanomamö:

> I looked up and gasped when I saw a dozen burly, naked, sweaty, hideous men staring at us down the shafts of their drawn arrows! Immense wads of green tobacco were stuck between their lower teeth and lips, making them look even more hideous, and strands of dark-green slime dripped or hung from their nostrils—strands so long that they clung to their pectoral muscles or drizzled down their chins.

Later Chagnon learns that just before his arrival, these men were battling rivals in a neighboring village—hence their hostility toward the pale-skinned stranger. Yanomamö males, as described by Chagnon, are almost comically violent. To resolve disputes or even just for sport, men in the same village whack each other over the head with clubs until one combatant quits or is knocked cold. Men display the lumps and scars on their heads like medals.

Yanomamö men from different villages also raid and kill each other with spears and bows and arrows. Fights are triggered by accusations of sorcery (which the Yanomamö believe causes most illnesses) and, even more commonly, disputes over women. Sometimes a man seduces, rapes, or kidnaps a female from another village, triggering a feud in which men kill to avenge past killings and scarcely remember how the war had started. By Chagnon's estimates, 30 percent of the male population dies violently.

Published at the Vietnam War's bloody peak, Chagnon's book seemed to undercut the proposition—often attributed to Rousseau—that prior to civilization humans were "noble savages" living in harmony with nature and each other. In 1988, Chagnon made headlines again with a paper published in *Science*. Yanomamö killers, he reported, have twice as many wives and three times as many children as non-killers, whom Chagnon—when I interviewed him for *Scientific American*—called "wimps." This finding seemed to imply that natural selection favored innately aggressive, warlike men in human prehistory.

Critics have accused Chagnon of exaggerating and even indirectly provoking Yanomamö violence. First, the visits by

Chagnon—or any outsiders—to the Yanomamö exposed them to pathogens to which they had little or no resistance. The Yanomamö blamed these illnesses on sorcery by their enemies, against whom they sought revenge. Second, Chagnon gave his favorite tribesmen machetes and other highly prized tools. Inevitably, Chagnon's critics charged, Yanomamö men vied for Chagnon's attention and gifts. In other words, they fought over access not to women—which Chagnon claims is the main cause of violence— but to Chagnon. Is it surprising that he recorded higher rates of violence than other anthropologists did?

On the other hand, the Yanomamö were apparently killing each other well before Chagnon arrived on the scene. A memoir by a white woman kidnapped and raised by the Yanomamö in the 1930s details raids and even massacres of women and children bloodier than anything reported by Chagnon. I found Chagnon's claims about the Yanomamö disturbing but persuasive, so much so that I wrote a positive account of his work for *Scientific American*.

WERE THE YANOMAMÖ TYPICAL?

This is the crucial question. Other studies—not just of living tribes but of ones that lived millennia ago—have suggested that the Yanomamö's violent behavior was all too typical of pre-state societies. The archaeological evidence for prehistoric warfare consists primarily of skeletons with crushed skulls, hack marks, and projectile points embedded in them; rock art depicting battles with spears, clubs, and bows and arrows; and walls and other fortifications that provide protection against attacks. Archaeologists have found these signs of prehistoric group violence throughout the world.

This ethnographic and archaeological research is summarized by the anthropologist Lawrence Keeley in his 1996 book *War Before Civilization: The Myth of the Peaceful Savage*, which like the work of Wrangham and Chagnon has become a touchstone in the debate over war's origins. In his book's introduction, Keeley reveals that he once assumed that war began with civilization. His research forced him to accept that the vast majority of pre-state societies waged war. The few exceptions proved the rule: nonviolent societies tended to be either pacified by other, more powerful groups or so geographically isolated that they never encountered potential enemies.

Keeley's most controversial claim is that war occurred even among the most primitive peoples known, nomadic hunter-gatherers, who traveled in search of their main sources of food: herds of animals and edible plants. Our ancestors were nomadic hunter-gatherers throughout the Paleolithic era, which began 2 million years ago. Then, about twelve thousand years ago, humans started cultivating crops and domesticating animals in permanent settlements. (Because they cultivate small gardens and live in semi-permanent villages, the Yanomamö represent a more advanced and, according to anthropologists such as Keeley, "modern" form of social organization than hunter-gatherers.)

Nomadic hunter-gatherers, also called foragers, are quite rare today. The best known are the !Kung, who live in the Kalahari desert in southern Africa. In her 1959 book *The Harmless People*, Elizabeth Marshall Thomas describes these bushmen as a gentle, jovial folk, "whose way of life had remained unchanged

for thousands of years." That noble-savage image was amplified
by the 1981 film *The Gods Must Be Crazy*, which depicts the
!Kung as innocents in the midst of an insane, violent, "civilized" world. But Keeley contends that in the nineteenth century the !Kung raided neighboring tribes before retreating to
their current home in the Kalahari desert. Hunter-gatherers on
other continents, he says, also battled: European colonizers of
Australia observed Aborigine hunter-gatherers fighting more
than two centuries ago, and ten-thousand-year-old rock drawings depict them throwing spears at each other.

Keeley rejects the claim of many previous anthropologists
that tribal combat usually took the form of ritualized games
with few casualties. Although warfare involved skirmishes and
ambushes rather than pitched battles, the fighting sometimes
culminated in massacres, in which one tribe wiped out all
members of a rival group. And the fighting, he argues, was
often chronic—over time the casualties piled up. War killed
25 percent of the population of prehistoric societies, Keeley
estimates, about the same rate that Chagnon observed among
the Yanomamö and more than ten times higher than the global
casualty rate during the blood-soaked twentieth century. Do
these data mean war is innate?

WAR'S RECENT ORIGIN

Chagnon and Keeley have persuaded me that people in simple,
tribal societies occasionally waged war before the emergence
of large, complex cultures. Hence we cannot blame war on
civilization in general or western civilization in particular, as

some scholars have. But neither Chagnon and Keeley nor any other researchers have established that war, in Barack Obama's words, "appeared with the first man." The *Homo* genus emerged about 2 million years ago and *Homo sapiens* about two hun dred thousand years ago. But the oldest clear-cut relic of lethal group aggression is not millions or hundreds of thousands of years old. It is a 13,000-year-old grave site along the Nile River in the Jebel Sahaba region of Sudan. Excavated in the 1960s, the site contains fifty-nine skeletons, twenty-four of which bear marks of violence, such as embedded projectile points.

What's more, the Jebel Sahaba site is an outlier. Most of the other evidence for warfare dates back no more than 10,000 years. The oldest known homicide victim—as opposed to war casualty—was a young man who lived 20,000 years ago along the Nile. The victim's skeleton has stone projectile points embedded in it. Evidence of earlier lethal violence is ambiguous at best. One frequently cited example is a 50,000-year-old male Neanderthal, found in a cave in Iraq, whose ribs were apparently pierced by a sharp object. The anthropologist Erik Trinkaus, who discovered the skeleton, thinks that the marks probably stemmed from an accident. "You find a lot of evidence of bumps and bruises and broken bones among Neanderthals and other early humans, Trinkaus says. Most of these injuries probably resulted from "hunting large animals who object to being speared."

Researchers have found the remains of *Homo sapiens*, Neanderthals, and *Homo erectus*—including a 780,000-year-old skeleton in Spain and a 600,000-year-old specimen in Ethiopia—that show signs of having been butchered with stone tools. These marks are consistent with cannibalism, but not necessarily with homicide, let alone warfare. The "defleshing" marks may be evidence of ritualistic treatment of the dead or of starvation-driven cannibalism, the anthropologist Tim White says, but they "cannot be considered evidence" for lethal group violence.

Sarah Blaffer Hrdy, an anthropologist and authority on both primates and early humans, believes that our human and proto-human ancestors were at least occasionally violent. Given how often fights occur among virtually all primates, including humans, "we can be fairly certain that lethal aggression occasionally broke out" in the Paleolithic era, she says. "It would be amazing if it did not." But Hrdy sees no persuasive evidence that war—which she defines as "organized aggression between groups with the intent of killing those in other groups"—is either ancient or innate.

Nomadic hunter-gatherers such as the !Kung "are known for being fiercely egalitarian and going to great lengths to downplay competition and forestall ruptures in the social fabric," she says. If disputes erupted between different bands, they would be far more likely to move on rather than risk their lives by fighting. Warfare emerged, Hrdy contends, when humans abandoned their foraging ways and settled down. Unlike nomadic hunter-gatherers, sedentary societies had assets worth fighting over, such as fertile land, fishing grounds, stored grains, and herds of animals. "As groups grow larger, less personalized, and more formally organized," Hrdy explains, "they would also be prone to shift from occasional violent disagreements between individuals to the groupwide aggression that we mistakenly take for granted as representative of humankind's naturally warlike state."

Defenders of the war-is-in-our-genes theory insist that absence of evidence of warfare deep in human prehistory does not equal evidence of absence, especially given the paucity of human and pre-human remains prior to ten thousand years ago. But archaeologists have found clear-cut relics of other complex cultural behaviors—big-game hunting, cooking, decoration of clothing, painting, music, religion, burials—dating back tens and even hundreds of thousands of years, so why not warfare? And if war is so hardwired, why does it break out only inter-mittently among pre-state societies as well as modern ones? Scientists believe that our capacity for language is innate, even hardwired, because all known human societies, the simplest and most complex, have employed language at all times. War, in contrast, comes and goes.

The sporadic nature of war leads even Keeley, whose work is often cited by proponents of genetic theories of warfare, to reject such theories. In a section of *War Before Civilization* titled "The Irrelevance of Biology," he acknowledges the "incredible plasticity" of human social behavior, noting that extremely bel-ligerent human societies can rapidly become peaceful, and vice versa. "To anthropologists," he writes, "who have spent over a century exploring the huge variety of human behavior and its mutability, human biology looks less like destiny and more like its absence."

Another surprising critic of genetic theories of warfare is Chagnon, chronicler of the Yanomamö. Chagnon often denounced critics of his work as left-wing, anti-war ideologues who denied any biological contributions to behavior, but he is far from being a genetic determinist. In his interviews with me, he consistently denied that Yanomamö males are compelled by their genes to wage war. Yanomamö males engage in raids and other violent behavior not because they are innately violent but because violent behavior is esteemed by their culture, Chagnon contends. Most village leaders resort to violence in a controlled manner, and males who cannot control their aggression generally do not live long enough to bear children. Many Yanomamö warriors have confessed to Chagnon that they loathe war and wish it could be abolished from their culture—and, in fact, in recent decades rates of violence have dropped dramatically as Yanomamö villages have, for better or worse, accepted mores of the outside world.

Chagnon once told me that if Yanomamö males were raised in a society that esteemed not violence but, say, farming skills, they would quickly conform to that system. I said he sounded like the evolutionary theorist Stephen Jay Gould, a fierce critic of genetic accounts of human violence and other behaviors. I meant to provoke Chagnon with the comparison, but to my surprise he did not object to it. "Steve Gould and I probably agree on a lot of things," he replied.

Still, war could be said to be biological in one simplistic sense: the vast majority of warriors in history and prehistory— more than 99 percent, according to one estimate—have carried a Y chromosome. Some men also seem especially predisposed to violence, including war. In the next chapter, I'll examine the possibility that innately bellicose men have helped perpetuate war since its emergence ten thousand years ago. I call this notion the "bad apples" theory of war.

CHAPTER TWO

You Can't Blame It All
on a Few Bad Apples

In January 2011, a local theater in my hometown sponsored a screening of *Restrepo*, a documentary about U.S. soldiers in Afghanistan, followed by a question and answer session with one of its makers, the journalist Sebastian Junger. Author of the best seller *The Perfect Storm* (turned into a film starring George Clooney), Junger is also an intrepid war correspondent. He first reported from a war zone, Bosnia, in 1993, and later he covered conflicts in Liberia, Sierra Leone, Nigeria, and Afghanistan, which he first visited in 1996.

In 2007 and 2008, Junger spent a total of five months embedded with an American platoon in the Korengal Valley, one of Afghanistan's most violent regions. Junger accompanied the soldiers as they built and defended a tiny outpost they named Restrepo, after a platoon member killed in action. Junger and a colleague, the photojournalist Tim Hetherington (who died in

2011 covering the conflict in Libya), recorded one hundred and fifty hours of video and turned it into a documentary.

Restrepo, which was nominated for an Academy Award, provides an almost unbearably intense immersion into the lives of combat soldiers. It is like a first-person shooter game, except with real bullets and blood. The film shows boyish soldiers wrestling and razzing each other between firefights, howling in grief after a buddy is killed, cheering after blasting an enemy soldier to bits. The documentary simply records these events, foisting no particular interpretation on us.

In his 2010 book *War*, Junger attempts to make sense of what he witnessed in Afghanistan, and he advances a dramatic explanation of war in general. Wars occur, Junger suggests, at least in part because males enjoy them. "War is a lot of things and it's useless to pretend that exciting isn't one of them," he writes. "It's insanely exciting." Junger claims that the "moral basis of the war doesn't seem to interest soldiers [in Afghanistan] much, and its long-term success or failure has a relevance of almost zero."

In an interview with the *Village Voice*, Junger is more explicit. "The politically incorrect truth," he says, "is that war is extremely ingrained in us—in our evolution as humans—and we're hardwired for it." As evidence for our predisposition for war, Junger cites the work of Wrangham, author of *Demonic Males*. In January 2011, I met Junger after a screening of *Restrepo* in my hometown. I confessed my belief that war might soon be abolished, and he gave me a quizzical look. He wished he shared my optimism, he replied, but his reporting and research had made him pessimistic about the prospects for long-term peace.

Junger is wrong that natural selection bred an affinity for war into our human and even pre-human ancestors, as I hope the previous chapter persuaded you. But could he be right that a subset of men find war "exciting" and are even "hardwired" for it? If so, that would make the challenge of abolishing war more daunting. There is certainly abundant anecdotal evidence that some men enjoy war—and I mean real war, not fictional representations of it in films and video games. The British historian Joanna Bourke has sifted through hundreds of first person accounts of combat by veterans of World Wars I and II and the Vietnam War, and these led her to conclude that many ordinary men take pleasure in combat, and specifically in killing.

"Indeed, it is not necessary to look for extraordinary personality traits or even extraordinary times to explain human viciousness," Bourke writes. She quotes a Belgian socialist, Henry de Man, who before fighting in World War I had thought himself "immune from this intoxication" of killing. While serving on an artillery crew, he recalls, he "secured a direct hit on an enemy encampment, saw bodies or parts of bodies go up in the air, and heard the desperate yelling of the wounded or the runaways. I had to confess to myself that it was one of the happiest moments of my life."

The journalist William Broyles Jr., who fought in Vietnam, revealed the pleasure he took from combat in his 1984 essay "Why Men Love War." He says that some men dislike talking about war not because they were traumatized by it, but because they "loved it." He likens the "great and seductive beauty" of killing to an ecstatic spiritual or sexual experience. Anecdotes like these—and humanity's bloody history—seem superficially to confirm the claim that at least some males are "bad apples" who enjoy hurting others.

HOW MOST SOLDIERS ACTUALLY FEEL ABOUT KILLING

Although some men enjoy war some of the time, studies of combat veterans suggest that most find war traumatic. As many as one in two soldiers involuntarily urinate or defecate when first plunged into a battle. During World War II, the U.S. armed forces screened potential draftees for mental fitness, and yet more than half a million soldiers—mostly men—suffered a psychological breakdown during the war.

In 1946, the psychiatrists Roy Swank and Walter Marchand reported that after thirty days of continuous fighting, most American infantrymen started showing signs of "combat exhaustion," including insomnia, tremors, and intense anxiety. After sixty days, 98 percent of the soldiers suffered full-blown psychiatric symptoms. Their thinking and responses to stimuli became sluggish and disordered. They became emotionally numb and apathetic, with some succumbing to a near-catatonic "vegetative phase."

Many men apparently fear killing as well as being killed. At the end of World War II, Samuel L.A. Marshall, a U.S. Army brigadier general and historian, polled four hundred companies of infantrymen who fought in Europe and the Pacific. He found that only 15 to 20 percent of the veterans fired their weapons in combat, even when ordered to do so. Marshall concluded that most soldiers have a profound aversion to taking a life. "The average and normally healthy individual," Marshall declares in his 1947 book *Men Against Fire*, "has such an inner and usually unrealized resistance toward killing a fellow man that he will not of his own volition take life if it is possible to turn away from that responsibility."

Critics have questioned whether Marshall surveyed as many troops as he claimed, but his results have been corroborated by reports from World War I, the American Civil War, the Napoleonic wars, and other conflicts. A survey of World War II fighter pilots found that most never shot down or even fired at an enemy plane. Less than 1 percent of the pilots accounted for 30 to 40 percent of the enemy planes destroyed. In an experiment carried out by the Prussian Army in the late eighteenth century, infantrymen struck a target seventy-five yards away with 60 percent of their shots. Yet in one battle, hundreds of Prussian soldiers shot only thirty-two Turkish troops at a distance of thirty paces. During the Battle of Wissembourg in 1870, French troops discharged 48,000 rounds but struck only 404 Germans. This "hit-ratio" of roughly one per one hundred rounds was typical of infantry battles in the eighteenth and nineteenth centuries—in part, perhaps, because many soldiers fired away from the enemy.

This remarkable evidence of soldiers' empathy for the enemy has been brought to light not by a pacifist scholar but by Dave Grossman, a former lieutenant colonel and Army Ranger and professor of psychology at West Point. In his books *On Killing* and *On Combat*, published in 1996 and 2004, Grossman emphasizes that for most men combat is hellish. Although many soldiers are initially exhilarated by killing the enemy, he says, later they often feel profound revulsion and remorse, which may mutate into post-traumatic stress disorder (PTSD) and other ailments. Psychological troubles experienced by many veterans are evidence of what Grossman calls a "powerful, innate human resistance toward killing one's own species."

This resistance can be overcome by intensified training, direct commands from officers, long-range weapons, and propaganda that glorifies the soldier's cause and dehumanizes the enemy. "With the proper conditioning and the proper circumstances, it appears that almost anyone can and will kill," Grossman writes. Indeed, General Marshall's report on low firing rates during World War II provoked the U.S. Army into revamping its training. Drill sergeants started ordering recruits to chant "kill, kill, kill" while exercising. Shooting drills conditioned soldiers to fire instantly and repeatedly at targets. The targets became much more realistic, with bull's-eyes replaced by man-shaped targets that in some cases squirted red paint when struck. More recently, the armed forces have begun training soldiers in computer-generated virtual realities that precisely reproduce combat conditions.

As a result of these and other changes in combat training, firing rates among infantrymen rose to 55 percent in the Korean War and as high as 90 percent in the Vietnam War. Grossman suspects that this surge in firing rates—together with the unpopularity of the war—contributed to the high rate of PTSD among Vietnam veterans. As many as 25 percent of the 2.8 million Americans who served in Vietnam displayed some symptoms of PTSD, including anxiety, depression, and substance abuse. A study released in 2007 concluded that 9 percent of all Vietnam veterans still suffer from persistent trauma.

RAND Corporation, a quasi-governmental think tank, reported in 2008 that almost 20 percent of veterans of Iraq and Afghanistan suffer from PTSD or depression. Sebastian Junger, following up on the soldiers he lived with in Afghanistan, found that many were haunted by their experiences there and sought solace in drugs and alcohol. Combat may excite some men some of the time, but it leaves many people scarred for life, further undermining Junger's claim that men are "hardwired" for war.

Junger is not the only war reporter to fear that we have a troubling affinity for war. Chris Hedges, who has witnessed war's horrors firsthand in Central America, the Middle East, and the former Yugoslavia, reached a similar conclusion in his 2003 book *War Is a Force That Gives Us Meaning*. He compares war to a potent drug to which many people, including himself, become addicted, because it "can give us purpose, meaning, a reason for living," and help us escape "the shallowness and vapidity of much of our lives." He fears that war "will always be part of the human condition."

I haven't experienced war as Hedges has, but I have an inkling of what he's talking about. On September 11, 2001, when I stood on a hill and saw smoke rising from the Manhattan skyline thirty miles south of my home, my fear and horror was tinged with a strange exhilaration at the sheer spectacle of the event. As I walked home, the trees, sky, and clouds seemed preternaturally bright, as if a veil that normally dims my vision had been torn away. Others have told me that they felt the same sensation that day.

So yes, war—like any cataclysmic event—can rip us out of

our daily routine and make us feel more alive, if only by reminding us of life's fleeting nature. As Hedges documents, war can
also test our courage and make us feel part of a grand narrative
that lifts us out of our relatively petty, humdrum concerns. My
grandfather re-enlisted in the Navy after Pearl Harbor, although
he was in his forties. After drifting through the Depression
without finding a satisfying job, he was, according to my father,
eager to feel the same sense of purpose that he had experienced
as a sailor during World War I.

But hurricanes, earthquakes, tsunamis, volcanoes, and other
disasters can evoke profound emotional reactions in us, and test
survivors' fortitude, and yet no sane person wants them to happen. Hedges knows as well as anyone that war, ultimately, does
not give us meaning. "War is brutal and impersonal," he writes.
"It mocks the fantasy of individual heroism and the absurdity
of utopian goals like democracy." War, in the end, annihilates
meaning, because it renders individual lives worthless. That is
why it traumatizes so many soldiers.

"THE 2 PERCENT WHO LIKE IT"

But what about those bad apples? A small subset of men do
indeed seem to take pleasure in war, including killing. Dave
Grossman notes that a few soldiers possess "the capacity for the
levelheaded participation in combat that we as a society glorify
and that Hollywood would have us believe that all men possess."
These are not, for the most part, crazed, compulsive killers but
rather men who "if pushed or if given a legitimate reason, will
kill without regret or remorse." They may be excellent soldiers

when well-trained and overseen by competent commanders, but they are also more likely than other men to use excessive force and commit atrocities.

Grossman calls these men "the 2 percent who like it." The 2 percent figure comes from the aforementioned finding by the psychiatrists Swank and Marchand that 98 percent of World War II veterans who endured sixty days of combat suffered a psychiatric breakdown. The flip side of this statistic is that 2 percent of the veterans, far from being traumatized by intense, prolonged combat, enjoyed it. Swank and Marchand diagnosed the soldiers in this group with "aggressive psychopathic personalities." To put it bluntly, combat didn't drive these men crazy because they were crazy to begin with.

Today, some psychiatrists prefer the slightly less derogatory terms "sociopathy" or "antisocial personality disorder" to psychopathy. These syndromes all refer to the same cluster of traits: extreme aggression, lack of empathy for others, and lack of remorse for one's actions. The *Diagnostic and Statistical Manual of Psychiatric Disorders* (*DSM*), which purports to reflect the consensus of American psychiatry, estimates that 3 percent of all males show symptoms of antisocial personality disorder and about half as many females. These percentages are suggestively close to Grossman's 2 percent figure.

Psychopaths lack the innate empathy that most humans— and even, to a lesser degree, chimpanzees and bonobos—start to display in childhood. Psychopaths "lie and manipulate yet feel no compunction or regrets—in fact, they don't feel particularly deeply about anything at all," write the neuroscientists Kent Kiehl and Joshua Buckholtz in a 2010 article in *Scientific American*.

Psychopaths not only lack empathy; they often have difficulty recognizing fearful or sad expressions in others. Psychotherapy, especially involving groups, is considered counterproductive for psychopaths, because "insights into others' vulnerabilities become opportunities to hone their manipulation skills," Kiehl and Buckholtz conclude. They estimate that as many as 35 percent of U.S. prisoners have psychopathic tendencies.

There is evidence that psychopathy—like schizophrenia, manic depression, autism, and other mental disorders—may be partially inherited. The Twins Early Development Study has tracked the progress of thousands of pairs of twins born in England between 1994 and 1996. In 2005 researchers asked teachers to fill out questionnaires about the behavior of 3,687 pairs of twins. About 5 percent of the children showed some degree of psychopathy. If one identical twin was psychopathic, the other was very likely to be as well; the correlation between fraternal twins was much smaller. The researchers estimated the heritability of psychopathy at 81 percent, roughly the heritability of height.

Some caveats: psychopathy is not a discrete syndrome, which you either have or don't have; it comes in degrees. And far from being compulsively violent, people with psychopathic traits can be quite successful, especially in fields that reward ruthlessness, such as business, law, and politics. As Grossman points out, men who lack empathy and remorse can make excellent soldiers; they are not all bloodthirsty maniacs.

It is nonetheless tempting to blame war and other forms of violence on a small number of psychopathic thugs, and there is even circumstantial support for that conjecture. The political scientist Bruce Jones, a former U.N. official, estimates that 2 percent of Hutu males above the age of thirteen carried out almost all of the genocide against Tutsis in Rwanda in the early 1990s. According to the political scientist Benjamin Valentino, small percentages of men—including leaders and soldiers—are responsible for much of the slaughter of the twentieth century, including mass killings in the Soviet Union, China, Cambodia, the Balkans, and Guatemala.

In her 2007 book *Evil Genes*, the biomedical engineer Barbara Oakley argues that Hitler, Stalin, Mao Zedong, and other notorious tyrants displayed symptoms of psychopathy. Hitler was apparently one of the 2 percent who like it. During World War I, he served in the 16th Bavarian Reserve, virtually every original member of which was wounded or killed. Hitler himself was wounded several times, but fought to the war's bitter end, and he later called his service in World War I "the greatest of all experiences."

But in the famous 1963 essay in which she coined the term "banality of evil," Hannah Arendt contends that Adolf Eichmann and other Nazi war criminals were "neither perverted nor sadistic" but "terribly and terrifyingly normal." George W. Bush and Vice President Dick Cheney, who led the U.S. into Afghanistan and Iraq, show no signs of a personal affinity for violence. Both men took pains to avoid serving in the Vietnam War. Bush did not even play competitive sports in college. He was a cheerleader. Neither of these men were bad apples, as I have defined the term, and yet they plunged the United States into two wars.

The cataclysmic wars and genocides of the twentieth century—and indeed all of human history and prehistory—demonstrate that, under the right circumstances, virtually anyone can act like a psychopathic killer. As Grossman notes, training and propaganda can overcome men's sympathy for and aversion to harming others. Neither psychopathy nor any other genetic explanation can account for war's emergence some ten thousand years ago, or its on-again-off-again pattern since then.

Genetic factors cannot even account for patterns of violent crime, which vary enormously both between different regions and over time in the same region. No purely biological model can explain why, for example, recent U.S. homicide rates are ten times lower than in El Salvador and ten times higher than in Japan.

THE WARRIOR GENE

These facts have not discouraged scientists from seeking genes that predispose some people to violence, nor have they stopped the media from hyping this research. In the 1960s, for example, British scientists claimed that men born with two Y chromosomes instead of one were prone to violent outbursts. This so-called "XYY syndrome" affects about one in every thousand men. The British study was based on nine men incarcerated in a mental hospital for violent patients. Other researchers, also focusing on institutionalized patients and criminals, quickly claimed to have found evidence that XYY men were hyper-aggressive "supermales" at risk of becoming violent criminals and even serial killers.

The XYY-supermale claim was propagated by the *New York Times* and other mainstream media, enshrined in biology and social science textbooks, and even written into plots for films, novels, and television shows. Meanwhile, follow-up studies of non-institutionalized XYY men failed to corroborate claims that they are prone to violence. In 1993, the National Academy of Sciences concluded after an exhaustive review that there is no correlation between the XYY syndrome and violent behavior.

By then, however, scientists were reporting a link between violent aggression and a gene on the X chromosome that produces the enzyme monoamine oxidase A (MAOA), which regulates the function of neurotransmitters such as dopamine and serotonin. The correlation first emerged from studies of a large Dutch family whose male members were mildly retarded and extremely violent. Two were arsonists, one tried to run over an employer with a car, another raped his sister and tried to stab the warden of a mental hospital with a pitchfork. The men all lacked monoamine oxidase A, suggesting that they possessed a defective version of the MAOA gene.

Many groups tried and failed to find this flawed version of the MAOA gene in other populations. In 2002, however, British researchers reported links between violent aggression and a common variant, or allele, of the MAOA gene, called MAOA-L, which produces low levels of the MAOA enzyme. The correlation was allegedly stronger if carriers had experienced some sort of trauma as children. Two follow-up studies failed to confirm the British group's claim, but again that did not stop the media from touting what was now being called "the warrior gene."

Race became a factor in warrior gene research in 2007, when geneticists in New Zealand reported that MAOA-L occurs in 56 percent of Maori men. "It is well recognized," the researchers commented, "that historically Maori were fearless warriors." The researchers' racial profiling was based on a study of forty-six men, who needed to have only one Maori parent to be defined as Maori. MAOA-L is reportedly less common among Caucasians (34 percent) and Hispanics (29 percent), but even more common among Africans (59 percent) and Chinese (77 percent).

In 2010, ABC News and other media hailed an experiment that supposedly demonstrated that MAOA-L carriers are "born to be violent," as a National Geographic broadcast put it. The experiment, carried out at Brown University, examines whether MAOA-L carriers are more likely than non-carriers to respond with "behavioral aggression" toward someone they think has cheated them out of money they had earned in a laboratory test. "Behavioral aggression" is defined as making the "cheater" consume hot sauce.

Even disregarding the issue of whether giving someone hot sauce counts as "physical aggression," the study provides little to no evidence for the warrior gene, since the difference between carriers and non-carriers is minuscule. The researchers examined seventy subjects, half of whom carried the warrior gene. Seventy-five percent of the warrior gene carriers "meted out aggression" when cheated—but so did 62 percent of the non-carriers. When subjects were cheated out of smaller amounts of money, there was no difference between the two groups.

The warrior gene just does not live up to its name. If it did, the whole world—and China in particular, if the racial statistics mentioned above are accurate—would be wracked by violence. My guess is that the warrior gene claims will eventually be discredited, because that's the pattern with attempts to link complex behavioral traits to specific genes. Over the last two decades, researchers have announced the discovery of "genes for" male homosexuality, religious belief, gambling, alcoholism, heroin addiction, novelty-seeking, impulsivity, anxiety, anorexia nervosa, and seasonal affective disorder as well as violent aggression. So far, not one of these claims has been confirmed by follow-up studies.

These failures should not be surprising, since all of these complex traits and disorders are almost certainly caused by many different genes interacting with many different environmental factors. Moreover, geneticists' methodology is highly susceptible to false positives. Researchers select a group of people who share a trait and then start searching for a gene that occurs not universally and exclusively, but simply more often in this group than in a control group. If you look at enough genes and traits, particularly poorly defined ones like "aggression," you will almost inevitably find a correlation simply through chance. Scientists will no doubt keep announcing—and the media will keep hyping—the discovery of genes that make some people "natural warriors" or "bad apples." But don't believe these claims or accept their implication that war and other forms of violence are biological problems.

Many pessimists, I suspect, adhere to the bad apple theory of warfare. They believe that war keeps breaking out because the worst among us, the bad apples, invariably drag the rest of us down to their level. The Yanomamö take this attitude, according to their chief chronicler, Napoleon Chagnon. "Almost everyone, including the Yanomamö, regards war as repugnant and would prefer that it did not exist," he writes. "Like us, they are more than willing to quit—if the bad guys also quit. If we could all get rid of the bad guys, there wouldn't be any war."

According to this view, even if the vast majority of us are decent, empathetic, and inclined toward peace, humanity will always be plagued by warmongers such as Genghis Khan, Hitler, and Osama bin Laden, who have violent ambitions and are charismatic enough to attract followers, who may be bad apples as well. We good guys, goes the thinking, must remain armed to protect ourselves against those bad guys, sometimes with preemptive attacks. By this logic, war and militarism will never end.

But this assertion does not withstand scrutiny. A few individuals do indeed seem to be incorrigibly aggressive, violent, and lacking in empathy for others. Bad apples. Fine. But war itself, rather than an innate lust for violence, turns most people into bad guys. When peace breaks out, bad guys are magically transformed into good guys, as history has demonstrated over and over again. England, France, Spain, Germany, and other European states clashed violently for centuries, but war between these members of the European Union has become unimaginable. My father, who as a young man fought the Japanese, now drives a Japanese car and watches a Japanese television. He and my sister Patty have vacationed in Vietnam, and my daughter Skye has a friend whose parents are Vietnamese American.

WHAT ABOUT BRAIN CHIPS, EMPOWERED WOMEN, OR OTHER BIO-SOLUTIONS?

Biological theories of war have inspired a slew of bio-solutions, which aim to repress, vent, or redirect our allegedly innate urge to fight. One of the most radical was proposed in the late 1960s by the Yale neurophysiologist José Delgado. Delgado, ironically, was one of the original signers of the Seville Statement, which repudiates biological theories of war. But he suggested that war and other forms of violence could be curbed by implanting radio-controlled electrodes in peoples' brains.

Delgado was the pioneer—and flamboyant promoter—of this technology. In 1963, he stood in a Spanish bullring as a bull with a radio-equipped array of electrodes implanted in its brain charged toward him. Delgado pushed a button on a radio transmitter, causing the "stimoceiver" to zap a region in the bull's brain supposedly associated with aggression. The bull stopped in its tracks and trotted away. The media marveled at Delgado's transformation of an aggressive beast into a real-life version of Ferdinand the Bull, the gentle hero of the popular children's story.

In other experiments, Delgado manipulated the limbs and emotions of cats, monkeys, chimpanzees, and humans (most of them mental patients) with implanted electrodes. In 1969, he extolled the potential benefits of brain-stimulation technologies, which would help us create "a less cruel, happier, and better man." In the 1970s, brain-implant research got bogged down in technical and ethical issues, but it has recently made a comeback, as scientists have begun exploring the potential of implanted devices for treating epilepsy, depression, paralysis, and other disorders of the nervous system. The Pentagon has become a major funder of research on brain-implant devices, which could in principle boost soldiers' physical and mental powers—and make them easier for commanders to control. This technology raises an obvious question: who gets the brain implant, and who gets the remote controller?

In the heyday of eugenics in the late nineteenth and early twentieth centuries, some scientists and commentators proposed that we reduce our aggression through selective breeding, just as breeders of dogs, cats, cattle, and other domestic animals have done. The Nazis gave eugenics a bad name, but recent research on genes associated with inherited diseases has resuscitated the idea that we can engineer ourselves to be nicer. Another possibility, say some, is pacifying people with drugs called serenics. One possible candidate is the hormone oxytocin, which has been linked to primates' feelings of affection and trust.

Other bio-solutions are cultural rather than strictly physiological. In his 1906 essay "The Moral Equivalent of War," William James suggests channeling young men's martial urges into a "war against nature," which would entail fishing, logging, digging tunnels, and other risky, invigorating work. The biologist and Nobel laureate Konrad Lorenz, in his 1963 book *On Aggression*, proposes that societies vent their aggression through "sporting contests" both within and between nations. Some scholars have taken this proposal seriously enough to test it, and they have found no correlation between societies' propensity for war and their fondness for sports.

If more sports doesn't make us less violent, what about more sex? During the 1960s, counterculture pundits claimed that imperialism, fascism, totalitarianism, and other forms of violent social control stemmed from repressed sexual desire. The implication of this hypothesis—expressed in the hippie slogan "Make love, not war"—was that more sex would mean less war. This meme has been revived by research on the sexy, peaceful bonobos. But there is no evidence that violent human societies engage in less sex than peaceful ones, or vice versa. If anything, some men and women find war sexually arousing.

The most serious bio-solution entails giving women more responsibility in contemporary human culture. Because innate male aggression is the primary cause of war, the reasoning goes, bestowing more political power on women will decrease the risk of war. But women are not innate pacifists any more than men are innate warriors. Joan of Arc, Queen Elizabeth I, Catherine the Great, Margaret Thatcher, Golda Meir, and Indira Gandhi were formidable war leaders. Although 99 percent of the combatants in all wars have been male, women can also make ferocious warriors if given the opportunity.

One remarkable example is a female regiment founded in the eighteenth century in the west African kingdom of Dahomey (now Benin). In 1727, a Dahomean king formed an all-female troop that included as many as six thousand women and lasted until 1892, when France conquered Dahomey. The women warriors were renowned for their courage and cruelty. Their favorite weapon was a gigantic folding razor with a blade over two feet long, with which these soldiers decapitated and castrated enemies.

During World War I, a Russian peasant named Maria Botchkareva organized a female "Battalion of Death" consisting of several hundred female soldiers. Russian leaders hoped that the female warriors would inspire, or shame, males to fight more boldly against the German Army. The tactic failed. The female fighters mounted several advances on German positions, but few of their exhausted, demoralized male comrades joined them. Botchkareva complained bitterly that "the men knew no shame."

Women have contributed to war indirectly as well. During World War I, women in England and America organized a campaign to shame men into joining the war effort. The women carried white feathers in their pockets and thrust them at men dressed in civilian clothes. After they received the vote in the U.S. and elsewhere, women did not favor less hawkish leaders and policies (as some male opponents of suffrage had feared).

The link between war and male dominance—like the link between war and every other factor—is tenuous. Some male-dominated societies are peaceful. Women only obtained the right to vote throughout war-averse Switzerland in the 1990s. Conversely, the United States has remained militaristic over the past century in spite of making progress in the direction of gender parity.

Biologically-based solutions cannot solve war, any more than biologically-based theories can explain it. "We would be lucky," the political scientist Joshua Goldstein remarks in his 2001 book *War and Gender*, to find that war is totally determined by our biology. We could just "find the hormone or neurotransmitter" that inhibits lethal behavior and "add it to the water supply like fluoride. (Instant peace, just add water.) Unfortunately, real biology is a lot more complicated and less deterministic." So the question remains: why did war begin in the first place? And what explains why it breaks out in certain times and places, but not in others?

CHAPTER THREE

Does Resource Scarcity Make Us Fight?
(No, Not Necessarily)

Entering the lobby of the Peabody Museum of Archaeology and Ethnology at Harvard University, you encounter a large glass case enclosing a fringed deerskin shirt. At first glance the shirt looks raggedy and unremarkable. But a closer look reveals faded embroidered images of men pierced by arrows, blood dripping from their wounds. According to a caption, Meriwether Lewis and William Clark collected this garment during their famous expedition across North America from 1804 to 1806. The shirt belonged to a warrior from a Northern Plains tribe, and each of these gory embroidered figures depicts one of his victories.

I think that Steven LeBlanc, director of collections at the Peabody, placed the shirt in the lobby to send a message: indigenous people in the Americas were killing each other before they made contact with Europeans. LeBlanc has adorned his office walls with more tribal war paraphernalia, including slings from Asia Minor and the Andes, body armor from New Guinea, and shields and spear-throwers from the Australian Outback. LeBlanc is bearded, barrel-chested, and heartily cheerful when denigrating those who view warfare as a relatively recent behavior. "Scholars who insist that war did not exist in the distant past," he says, have "no interest in getting to the real evidence."

Like his Harvard colleague Richard Wrangham, LeBlanc is an adamant advocate of the view that war is ancient and innate. In his 2003 book *Constant Battles: Why We Fight*, co-written with the journalist Katherine Register, LeBlanc calls war "a common and almost universal human behavior that has been with us as we went from ape to human." But LeBlanc blames war primarily on demographic and environmental factors—in particular the tendency of a population to outgrow its environment's capacity to nourish everyone.

"Since the beginning of time," he writes, "humans have been unable to live in ecological balance. No matter where we happen to live on Earth, we eventually outstrip the environment. This has always led to competition as a means of survival, and warfare has been the *inevitable* consequence of our ecological-demographic propensities." I italicized "inevitable" to show how deterministic LeBlanc's view is. Warfare invariably erupts, he believes, as a result of population surges, droughts, and other conditions that lead to scarcity of food. During the modern era, he says, the primary focus of armed conflict has simply shifted from food to energy sources, notably fossil fuels.

LeBlanc's explanation of war is basically the "war-is-in-our-genes" thesis plus a dose of Thomas Malthus. A British clergyman and scholar, Malthus based what he called his "melancholy" theory on two axioms: "First, That food is necessary to the existence of man. Secondly, That the passion between the sexes is necessary." Malthus predicted that population, "when unchecked," will rapidly outpace the Earth's food-producing capacity. As a result, he said, many humans would die prematurely as a consequence of famine, disease, and fighting. This hypothesis, published in 1798, inspired Darwin's theory of natural selection, which assumes that all creatures produce excess offspring, only the fittest of which survive long enough to reproduce.

Malthusian theories of war are quite popular. In his 822-page book *War in Human Civilization*, published in 2006, the Israeli political scientist Azar Gat weighs countless theories of warfare's causation before finally favoring "the competition over scarce resources." In principle, this view should perhaps engender more optimism than purely biological theories. Malthusian models imply that humans wage war not simply because their genes compel them to do so but for rational reasons: societies fight for survival and security. This perspective, in fact, gives LeBlanc confidence that we can overcome war. Two key steps to reducing war's probability, he claims, are controlling population growth and finding alternatives to fossil fuels. "I was just in Germany," LeBlanc informed me happily, "and there are windmills everywhere!"

But what if we cannot curb our population growth and consumption of fossil fuels and other resources quickly enough, or at all? Does that mean we are doomed to wage war? Many pundits on the left and right seem to think so. They warn that global warming—unless we take drastic steps to stop it—will trigger catastrophic conflicts. I understand these concerns. According to some climate forecasts, surging sea levels and intensifying storms might create an enormous refugee crisis by driving people from low-lying coastal lands. Even more worrisome is the fact that climate change might produce worldwide shortages of fresh water. Climatologists predict that droughts will become more frequent and intense, already dry regions will become more parched, and water supplies from seasonal snowmelts will diminish or even vanish.

Many of the world's poorest people now lack clean water for drinking, sanitation, and agriculture, and water disputes are already exacerbating tensions in troubled regions. Israel controls rivers and aquifers upon which Palestinians and Jordanians depend. Pakistan fears that the water it needs for agriculture will be reduced by a dam project in India. India in turn is anxious about dam projects in China. African countries bordering the Nile are bickering over water rights. Droughts are thought to be exacerbating lethal conflicts in the Sudan and other African nations, which also have some of the world's fastest-growing populations. Global warming could make such conflicts "more rather than less likely," the British home secretary John Reid stated in 2006. The environmental scientist Lester Brown, founder of the respected Worldwatch Institute, warns that unless we drastically reduce our carbon emissions and population growth, "civilization itself could disintegrate."

One of the ironies of the recent Bush administration is that while officials like Vice President Dick Cheney downplayed global warming, the Pentagon was quietly concluding that it posed a tremendous threat to security. One Defense Department study concluded that climate change could trigger "desperate, all-out wars over food, water, and energy supplies." The study asserts that "wars over resources were the norm until about three centuries ago. When such conflicts broke out, 25 percent of a population usually died. As abrupt climate change hits home, warfare may again come to define human life." As evidence for this thesis, the study cited the writings of "Harvard archaeologist Steven LeBlanc."

THE CIRCUMSCRIPTION THEORY OF WAR

I reject the view that scarcity of resources leads "inevitably," as Steven LeBlanc puts it, to warfare. Clearly, we must find more sustainable means of living, for the sake of humanity and the rest of nature. But our history and prehistory simply do not support the pessimistic conclusion that resource scarcity and war are inevitably or inextricably connected. Malthusian factors have played a role in some conflicts, but not in others. Again, war cannot be pinned on any one definite cause.

But before showing the flaws of the Malthusian explanation of war, let me give it its full due. As I point out in chapter one, war arose not millions of years ago (as LeBlanc claims) but less than twelve thousand years ago, as our ancestors started abandoning their nomadic ways and settling down in lands with plentiful game, edible plants, and water. Populations surged in these regions as people domesticated animals and cultivated wild cereals and other crops on fertile land surrounding major rivers—notably the Tigris, Euphrates, Nile, Indus, and Yellow. Farmers accumulated surplus food, crafted increasingly sophisticated tools, and built permanent dwellings out of wood and stone, all of which meant they had more worth stealing or defending.

For most of human prehistory, people could simply walk away from disputes, because land was so plentiful. But according to the "circumscription theory" of the origin of civilization, proposed by the anthropologist Robert Carneiro in 1970, some especially fertile regions were bounded by mountain ranges, deserts, seas, or other geographical obstacles that made dispersal difficult, if not impossible. Within these regions, small farming communities began to fight, conquer, and form alliances with each other. In this way, Carneiro suggests, villages merged into chiefdoms, which in turn fused into the first great civilizations in Mesopotamia, Egypt, India, and China, and later in Mesoamerica and the Andes.

Ancient states, as described by Carneiro, resembled protection rackets. Powerful warlords promised to protect people from famine and violence in exchange for labor, military service, taxes, and other payments. And they killed those who spurned their offer. In other words, the warlords represented the primary threat to the people they protected. "Force, and not enlightened self-interest, is the mechanism by which political evolution has led, step by step, from autonomous villages to the state," Carneiro writes.

Mesopotamia, Egypt, and other primordial states boosted agricultural production by constructing large-scale irrigation systems, as well as roads and storage facilities. Yet states and smaller societies still often outgrew the capacity of their lands to support them. Some brought on their own problems by over-farming, over-grazing, and over-foresting, and others were felled by a shift in climate that diminished food production. Self-induced ecological damage plus a long-term drought are thought to have contributed to the collapse of the Mayan civilization in Mesoamerica and the Anasazi culture in the southwest United States.

These examples would seem to lend support to the Malthusian theory. So do some smaller-scale societies, such as the Chumash, hunter-gatherers who settled along the coast of southern California as early as ten thousand years ago. Chumash skeletons dating back thousands of years—well before the arrival of Europeans—display signs of violence, including skull fractures and embedded arrow and spear points. Analysis of tree rings and other evidence indicate that fighting among the Chumash escalated during periods of drought.

A different sort of climate change destroyed a once-thriving Norse culture in Greenland. Norse sailors colonized the island in the tenth century CE and built a replica of their homeland, complete with farmland, pastures for cattle and other livestock, stone houses, and churches. In retrospect, the community benefited from several centuries of relatively warm weather in the northern hemisphere. But it could not survive the Little Ice Age, a cold spell that froze Europe and the North Atlantic in the fourteenth century. Excavations of the Norse settlements reveal violence in the society's twilight.

Even the Crusades, the quintessential religious conflict, could be said to stem in part from Malthusian conditions. By the eleventh century, most European landowners practiced primogeniture, bequeathing their estates to their first born sons;

this custom had produced a large population of rootless young men, many of whom had trained to be knights. These knights offered their martial services to whomever would pay them. In 1095, Pope Urban II issued the following proclamation to these warriors:

> "For this land which you now inhabit, shut in on all sides by the sea and the mountain peaks, is too narrow for your large population; it scarcely furnishes food enough for its cultivators. Hence it is that you murder and devour one another, that you wage wars, and that many among you perish in civil strife. Let hatred, therefore, depart from among you; let your quarrels end. Enter upon the road to the Holy Sepulcher; wrest that land from a wicked race, and subject it to yourselves."

Thus did Pope Urban launch the First Crusade, in a speech that anticipated Malthus and even circumscription theory. The Pope's letter seems to support LeBlanc's claim that competition for resources fuels conflicts that on the surface seem to have religious, political, or ethnic bases.

MALTHUSIAN EXCEPTIONS

But other examples contradict the Malthusian model of war. The anthropologist Keith Otterbein notes that some early agricultural societies—even in circumscribed areas subject to population pressure—lived peacefully for centuries or longer. One of the oldest known settlements was Abü Hureyra, near

the Euphrates River. Excavations have revealed that people
began erecting permanent dwellings and cultivating grains in
this fertile region 11,500 years ago. Life wasn't easy; bones of
male and female inhabitants show signs of hard labor and disease. But for more than four thousand years, generations came
and went with no signs of warfare. And contrary to the claim
of Carneiro that the first city-states were founded through violent conquest, ancient Sumerian cities like Ur and Uruk, in
eastern Mesopotamia, thrived for centuries before constructing
fortifications and amassing armies. Archaeological digs reveal a
similar pattern in the evolution of primordial agricultural societies in China and the Americas, which were circumscribed and
densely populated but did not engage in significant warfare for
many generations after being founded.

Conversely, some simple tribal societies fought in the *absence*
of dense population and deprivation. To wit, Australian Aborigines were nomadic hunter-gatherers, not farmers, and yet ten
thousand years ago they carved rock drawings that seem to depict
them battling each other. Indeed, some tribal people recognized
war as a *cause* of scarcity rather than vice versa. One warrior in
New Guinea told an ethnographer: "War is bad and nobody likes
it. Sweet potatoes disappear, pigs disappear, fields deteriorate,
and many relatives and friends get killed."

Napoleon Chagnon has always adamantly denied that the
Yanomamö fought over land, game, and other resources. If anything, he argues, Yanomamö warfare is more intense in areas
with the sparsest populations and most plentiful food. "If one
insists on a narrow cause-effect relationship between warfare
intensity and protein consumption," Chagnon writes, "a much

stronger case could be made that those people who have the highest levels of protein consumption are the ones who are the most warlike."

All these cases suggest that there is no clear-cut correlation between resource scarcity and warfare. So does a comprehensive study of a wide range of societies carried out by the anthropologists Carol and Melvin Ember. For decades, this husband and wife team oversaw the Human Relations Area Files, which contains detailed information gathered over the past two centuries on more than three hundred and sixty simple and complex societies.

When I interviewed them in their offices at Yale University, they kept interrupting, challenging, and correcting each other. But they agreed that their cross-cultural analysis generates several significant conclusions. First, war is not restricted to states, chiefdoms, and other complex societies; some hunter-gatherers have clearly waged war, although others have never been observed fighting or do so only occasionally. The enormous variability of warfare both within and between cultures, Melvin said, suggests that "we are not dealing with genes or a biological propensity" for war.

The Embers also turned up no evidence for the scarce-resources theory of war. Melvin was initially inclined to believe the theory, because in the 1980s he found a link between population density and warfare among tribal New Guineans who practiced small-scale farming. The victors in war typically seized land from losers. But when Carol and Melvin examined 186 cultures from all over the world, they did not find support for the scarce-resources theory, at least not in its simplest form.

The cultures, which represent different historical periods and levels of social development, include ancient civilizations such as the Babylonians, Aztecs, and Romans; hunter-gatherers such as the Aleut and !Kung; more complex tribal societies such as the Maori and Yanomamö; and even modern ethnic groups such as the Albanians and Kurds.

War among these cultures did not break out, according to the Embers, as populations surged and subside as populations fell. Nor was there a correlation between warfare and persistent scarcity of food and other resources. "Chronic scarcity has no effect whatsoever on warfare frequency," Carol told me. What the Embers did find was something more subtle. The strongest correlates of warfare were unpredictable natural disasters—floods, droughts, earthquakes, insect infestations—that had disrupted food supplies in the past.

The Embers are careful to note that it is not the disasters themselves that precipitated war, but the memory of past disasters and hence the fear of future ones. This is a key point. The Embers write: "Societies with only the threat of disasters, with a memory of unpredictable disasters but no actual disasters during a twenty-five-year period, fought very frequently."

In other words, wars stemmed from factors that were not demographic and ecological so much as psychological. If a war to avoid imminent starvation is a war of necessity, most wars were not wars of necessity. They were wars of choice, motivated by a fear of the possibility of scarcity. What's most disconcerting, I think, about the fear-of-scarcity motive is that it can apply to any society at any time. No matter how prosperous we are, we can always imagine some disaster—including, of course, war itself—that will strip us of everything. So we go to war, which, ironically, often inflicts on us a disaster worse than what we feared.

Fear—as well as ambition and greed —no doubt motivated some ancient chiefs, kings, and emperors to keep expanding their forces, both to conquer new lands and maintain order within their borders. Hence an increasing proportion of a society's human power was diverted from farming to fighting. As a result, food production per capita dropped, leading to greater shortages and social unrest, which provoked rulers into building up their forces further and repressing civilians more violently. Scholars such as the economist Thomas Homer-Dixon have shown that this destabilizing cycle—in which warfare exacerbates resource scarcity which in turn instigates more war—contributed to the collapse of a wide variety of ancient societies, from the Roman and Mayan empires to the chiefdoms of Easter Island.

PROS AND CONS OF THE
INDUSTRIAL REVOLUTION

Fear of scarcity has motivated some modern nations to wage war. The desire to secure resources, especially fossil fuels, played a role in imperial Japan's violent conquests in the 1930s, Iraq's invasion of Kuwait in 1990, and the counter-attack by the U.S. a year later. But actual scarcity of resources (as opposed to fear of future scarcity) explains modern international warfare even less than it explains pre-state conflicts.

That may be because modern states have been astonishingly successful at escaping what some scholars have called the

"Malthusian trap." Through most of our history, the vast majority of humanity lived a hand-to-mouth existence; only a minuscule elite was wealthy. Average standards of living remained stagnant for the first millennium CE, and rose only slightly over the next eight hundred years. In 1800, the average income in Western Europe was slightly less than the average income in modern Africa, the world's poorest region.

Since then, however, the percentage of humanity living in poverty has fallen dramatically. About one sixth of the global population, or 1.4 billion people, now survive on less than $1.25 a day, the U.N.'s definition of "extreme poverty." (The U.S. definition of poverty for Americans is less than $30 a day.) The number of extremely poor people is shamefully high, and yet as a percentage of the population it is extremely low compared to historical levels. Over the past two centuries the world's population has grown six fold and per-capita income has grown nine-fold, contradicting Malthus's dire forecasts. Per capita income has skyrocketed in Europe and the United States, by fifteen-fold and twenty-five-fold. Meanwhile, life expectancies have doubled as a result of public-health measures to almost seventy years—almost eighty in first-world nations such as Japan and the U.S.

Our material progress can be traced back to the Industrial Revolution, which began in Europe and jump-started a global economic surge that continues to this day. The Industrial Revolution generated a host of productivity-boosting innovations: steam engines, railroads, mechanized looms, cotton gins, nitrogen-based fertilizers, telegraphs, light bulbs, and gasoline-powered automobiles, trucks, and farm equipment.

Unlike finite resources such as gold, oil, and land, most scientific innovations can in principle be infinitely replicated (albeit limited by, say, fuel needs and materials). Hence they rapidly spread around the world, yielding economic benefits that spur further innovation and growth.

Contrary to complaints by critics of capitalism and imperialism, economic growth has not been an entirely zero-sum game, in which the wealthy and powerful prosper at the expense of the poor. In fact, the "Green Revolution," which boosted agricultural production in third-world countries, demonstrates how prosperous nations can help developing ones: in the 1940s, the Rockefeller Foundation funded research to find higher-yield varieties of grain. The program helped transform Mexico, the first test bed for the new crops, from a net importer of grain to an exporter in just twenty years. Later, India multiplied its wheat production five-fold in thirty years, outpacing its population growth.

Unfortunately, the decline in poverty over the past two centuries has not been matched by a comparable decline in militarism and war, a fact that pokes a hole in the Malthusian explanation of war's roots. The Industrial Revolution gave us industrial war, in which we fought with machine guns, tanks, bombers, battleships, poison gas, and nuclear bombs. World Wars I and II embroiled the world's most prosperous nations. These terrible conflicts often resulted in food shortages, especially among the poor and powerless. In her 2010 book *Churchill's Secret War*, the journalist Madhusree Mukerjee provides overwhelming documentary evidence that in the early 1940s, at least 3 million Indians starved to death as a direct result of England's diversion of grain from India to British civilians and troops. Another case of war causing scarcity rather than vice versa.

THE STATISTICS OF DEADLY QUARRELS

Malthus's "melancholy" theory certainly provides insights into the history of humanity. His timing was terrible, however, because almost as soon as he had proposed his idea, humanity started proving that it could escape the boom-bust cycles of population surges and crashes. And yet war continued.

Malthus was hardly alone in proposing an economic explanation for conflict. In the mid-nineteenth century, an obscure German scholar living in London—ground zero of the Industrial Revolution—proposed a rival theory. The cause of conflict, Karl Marx proposed, was not scarcity per se, but economic inequality, which was the inevitable consequence of capitalism and other economic systems based on private ownership. As long as capitalism persists, Marx predicted, so will war between haves and have-nots. Communism has not exactly solved the problem of war, any more than capitalism has, but could Marx's explanation of conflict be correct?

One of the most rigorous attempts to test theories of war—including those of Malthus and Marx—was carried out in the middle of the last century by the British physicist Lewis Fry Richardson. Richardson spent his early career as a weather researcher for the British Meteorological Service. His 1922 book *Weather Prediction by Numerical Process* laid the foundation for modern forecasting and anticipated many of the concepts and methods of chaos theory.

A pacifist and conscientious objector, Richardson served on a Quaker ambulance unit during World War I. In 1920, fearing that the military would use his forecasts for planning poison-gas attacks, he resigned from the British Meteorological Service when it became a branch of the British Armed Forces. For the rest of his life, Richardson studied war, modeling it with the same mathematical methods with which he had analyzed weather. He compiled data on war from an enormous number of sources, ranging from the *Encyclopedia Britannica* to newspapers and obscure political journals. He was still working on his magnum opus, *The Statistics of Deadly Quarrels*, when he died in 1953. Quincy Wright, another war scholar, edited Richardson's manuscript and got it published in 1960.

Deadly Quarrels lists and analyzes hundreds of lethal conflicts that occurred from 1815 through 1945, ranging from homicides perpetrated by criminal gangs up to the First and Second World Wars. Other major "quarrels" include China's Taiping Rebellion of 1851 to 1864, in which as many as 20 million people died; the Great War in La Plata of 1865-1870, which culminated in the extermination of more than 80 percent of Paraguayans; and the Zulu revolt against the British in 1906.

Richardson devotes a chapter to economic causes of war, including those postulated by Malthus and by Marx. Richardson finds that, contra Marx, "rich and poor were usually intermingled" on each side of a conflict, including the Russian Revolution itself. Richardson searches for evidence of other possible overriding economic factors, such as taxation, population pressure, restrictions on trade or migration, the desire for new territory, and what he calls the "fall from comfort into poverty." Because he identifies multiple causes for individual wars, Richardson comes up with a list of 244 causes for eighty-three major wars. Only 29 percent of the 244 causes are economic, and economics played no role at all in almost one third of the wars. Nor does Richardson find evidence that population growth increased the risk of conflict. In short, his massive statistical analysis provides scant support for Marxist or Malthusian explanations of war.

ECO-SOLUTIONS TO WAR FALL SHORT

In chapter two, I noted that biological theories of war have inspired "bio-solutions," ranging from brain implants that suppress violent impulses to sporting events that might vent aggression. In the same way, Marxist and Malthusian theories have inspired solutions that counteract supposed ecological and economic causes of war. Let's call these "eco-solutions."

One eco-solution entails reducing violence through socialism. The psychologists Margo Wilson and Martin Daly, for instance, have sought to explain why Canada's homicide rate is only about a third of that in the States, and why rates of homicide vary widely from region to region within each country. The best predictor of high homicide rates in a region, Daly and Wilson assert, is income inequality. As a measure of such inequality, Daly and Wilson employ the so-called Gini index (named after its originator, the Italian statistician Corrado Gini), which ranks inequality on a scale ranging from 0.0 to 1.0. A region in which everyone has exactly the same income would have a Gini score of 0.0, whereas a region in which one person makes all the money would have a score of 1.0.

Daly and Wilson find a strong correlation between high Gini scores and high homicide rates in Canadian provinces and U.S. counties. High Gini scores serve as better predictors of deadly violence than low average income or high unemployment do. Basically, Daly and Wilson are blaming homicides not on poverty, exactly, but on the ancient tug of war between haves and have-nots. The income-inequality hypothesis, Daly and Wilson contend, can account for the "radically different national homicide rates" in the U.S. versus Canada. Canada, after all, has broader social-welfare programs and hence fewer economic disparities than the United States. The implication of their hypothesis is that societies can reduce homicide rates via a more equitable economic system, perhaps with higher taxes for the wealthy and more generous welfare programs for the poor.

While these programs are, I believe, worth pursuing in and of themselves, scholars examining other nations around the world have found less evidence linking economic inequality to homicides. And of course some socialist leaders, notably Stalin, Mao, and even Hitler, who built political support for the Nazi party with generous welfare programs, have carried out appalling crimes against humanity.

The economist Jeffrey Sachs holds that the best way to reduce war, terrorism, and other forms of violence is to reduce poverty, and the best way to reduce poverty is via "capitalism with a human face." In the late 1990s, Sachs helped U.N. officials design the Millennium Development Goals, a plan for eliminating extreme poverty. The plan calls for affluent nations to give impoverished countries grants for education, healthcare, transportation, and communication. Then, according to Sachs, business investments plus international aid, which Sachs calls "Enlightened Globalization," could help these regions become self-sufficient.

I agree with Sachs that affluent nations have a moral obligation to help those mired in poverty. But I don't share his confidence that globalization and aid alone will reduce conflicts fueled by religious, ethnic, and political divisions. Even Sachs acknowledges that economic development conducted in the name of globalization often makes the rich richer and the poor poorer—and incites conflict. In northern India, for example, the government has forced thousands of poor farmers off their land to make way for a multinational aluminum-mining operation, triggering violent protests met with even more violent government crackdowns.

I also have doubts about a different eco-solution to war proposed by the journalist and environmental activist Bill McKibben. In his 2010 book *Eaarth* (the extra "a" indicates our planet's irrevocably altered nature), McKibben argues that unchecked global warming will plunge us into wars over water, food, and other necessities. He cites, among other sources, the Pentagon report that I mentioned earlier in this chapter. To avoid this fate, he says, we need to reject globalization and big government and create small, self-sustaining communities that generate their own energy, grow their own organic food, and even organize their own militias for self-defense.

Although I agree with McKibben that we need to cut back on our consumption of fossil fuels and other resources, I don't think we need to scale back civilization to accomplish that goal. Big government and big business, in spite of their manifest flaws, have their upsides. The Clean Water and Air Acts, the Endangered Species Act, and other federal laws and regulations have helped clean up the environment. In the 1980s, the Hudson River was filthy, filled with sewage and industrial toxins. But I have been swimming in it with my kids since the late 1990s. The air in New York City is much cleaner than it was decades ago. Multinational corporations have brought us green technologies like the Prius (which gets more than forty miles per gallon) and are rapidly improving the efficiency of solar and wind energy.

All eco-solutions, in the end, rest on a flawed assumption: that resource scarcity equals war. On the other hand, as the Embers have shown, *fear* of scarcity—and fear of war itself—can indeed provoke war. I'm thus concerned about the warnings of McKibben and other green activists, the pronouncements that unless we take drastic steps to change our behavior we will descend into violent, civilization-destroying chaos. Rather than inspiring people to install solar panels, grow their own vegetables, and support federal research on clean energy, these alarming prophesies might provoke people into supporting higher defense budgets and even stockpiling firearms as protection against the impending apocalypse. In this way, prophesies of wars over water, food, and other resources could become self-fulfilling.

THE ESSENTIAL MYSTERY OF WAR

The British historian John Keegan, one of the world's leading authorities on war, notes that theories of war generally fall into one of two categories. On one side are "naturalist" explanations, which attribute lethal group conflict to innate factors. On the other side are "materialist" theories, which blame conflict on economic and ecological factors. I think that neither naturalist nor materialist explanations really capture war's complexity.

Scholars have sought other explanations that can supplement if not replace naturalist and materialist theories. Carol and Melvin Ember, for example, investigated whether societies that encourage young boys to be tough and physically aggressive tend to be more warlike, but warfare seems to promote cultural machismo rather than vice versa. Lewis Fry Richardson turned up little support for other popular theories. Arms races are not strongly correlated with wars, nor do trade or a shared language make nations less likely to fight. Richardson reported two statistically significant, but not terribly surprising patterns: neighbors are more likely to fight each other than non-neighbors, and new wars are more likely to break out in the vicinity of warring regions.

Richardson's statistics display a Poisson distribution, a mathematical function that describes phenomena whose amplitude is inversely proportional to their frequency, but that otherwise occur in a random fashion. Earthquakes, storms, and floods all conform to Poisson distributions—and so do wars, according to Richardson's data. His conclusions corroborate a 1957 study by the Russian American sociologist Pitirim Sorokin, who sees no clear-cut pattern in outbreaks of war going back as far as 500 BCE Wars, overall, are not associated with any particular type of culture, or with economic expansion or decline.

These analyses highlight the essential mystery of war. Researchers have desperately searched for war's causes, but they have found both too many and too few. War has been blamed on a dizzying array of factors, but wars are so diverse that you can find evidence to support or contradict almost any theory. War has even been blamed on the desire for peace! The historian David Bell points out that many modern leaders—from Napoleon to Woodrow Wilson—have waged war with the stated goal of attaining universal peace. "Dreams of an end to war may be as unexpectedly dangerous as they are noble," Bell writes, "because they seem to justify almost anything done in their name."

Many conditions appear to be sufficient for war to occur, but none are necessary. Some societies remain peaceful even when significant risk factors are present, such as high population density, resource scarcity, and economic and ethnic divisions between people. Conversely, other societies fight in the absence of these conditions. Which leads us to the next question: how can this complex pattern of social behavior possibly be explained?

CHAPTER FOUR

Is War a Cultural Contagion? (Yes)

I once posted on the internet a list of what I called the "Greatest Science Books." A more accurate title would have been "Science Books John Horgan Happens to Own and Like." My inclusion of *Coming of Age in Samoa* by Margaret Mead provoked the most agitated responses. One commenter accused Mead of "lying and distorting the facts" about Samoa. Another pointed out that the Intercollegiate Studies Institute, a group of conservative academics, had declared that *Coming of Age* was the *worst* book of the twentieth century. The Institute stated: "Mead misled a generation into believing that the fantasies of sexual progressives were an historical reality on an island far, far away."

Mead was indeed nurtured in a progressive milieu. Her parents were both Quakers and social scientists, and Mead studied anthropology at Barnard under Ruth Benedict and Franz Boas, who were staunch opponents of genetic theories of human nature.

With their encouragement, in 1925 Mead set out to do fieldwork on the Polynesian island of Samoa. *Coming of Age in Samoa* made Mead famous after its publication in 1928, when she was only twenty-seven. As described by Mead, young Samoans engaged in sex with little guilt and jealousy and with many partners before settling down happily to have children.

The book is a not-so-implicit critique of western sexual mores, which according to Mead inflict needless suffering on young men and women. *Coming of Age* also represents a rebuke to social Darwinism, eugenics, and other ideologies that emphasized genetic determinants of human behavior and social structures. The meta-theme of *Coming of Age* (and all Mead's writings) is that we have more power to choose our destinies than we may think. The way things are is not the way things must or should be.

Mead remains a frequent target not only of conservatives, but also of scientists who emphasize genetic contributions to human behavior, including war. The psychologist Steven Pinker faults her for implying that human minds are "blank slates" unconstrained by biology. Richard Wrangham accuses Mead of claiming that "human evil is a culturally acquired thing, an arbitrary garment that can be cast off like our winter clothes."

These criticisms are unfair. First of all, Mead is no blank-slater. She repeatedly acknowledges that we are biological creatures, and that behavioral differences between the two sexes, as well as individuals, stem at least in part from genetic differences. She merely insists that our biology allows us more degrees of freedom than we often realize—and more than some scientists claim. Also, Mead's explanation of the complex, on-again-off-again pattern of war is far more persuasive than the theories of genophiles like Pinker and Wrangham.

Mead's most succinct account of war is her 1940 essay "Warfare is Only an Invention—Not a Biological Necessity." Mead begins by dismissing the notion that war is the inevitable consequence of any so-called "basic, competitive, aggressive, warring human nature." This claim is contradicted, she notes, by the simple fact that not all societies wage war. War has never been observed among a Himalayan people called the Lepchas or among the Eskimos. In fact, these groups, when questioned by early ethnographers, were puzzled by the very concept of war. "The idea of war is lacking," Mead writes, "and this idea is as essential to really carrying on war as an alphabet or a syllabary is to writing."

In discussing the Eskimos, Mead distinguishes between individual and group violence. Eskimos are "not a mild and meek people," she notes. Far from being natural pacifists, they engage in "fights, theft of wives, murder, and cannibalism," apparently sometimes provoked by fear of starvation. "The personality necessary for war, the circumstances necessary to goad men to desperation are present, but there is no war." Having disposed of biological explanations, Mead next turns to social and economic ones, including those implied by the theories of Malthus and Marx. Is war the inevitable consequence of dense populations and resource scarcity? The struggle between haves and have-nots? The competition between complex societies, especially states?

Just as the biological theory of war is contradicted by simple societies that don't fight, Mead asserts, so this theory of "sociological inevitability" is belied by simple societies that do fight. Hunter-gatherers on the Andaman Islands "represent an exceedingly low level of society," Mead writes, but they have been observed waging wars, in which "tiny army met tiny army in open battle." Australian Aborigines, similarly, occasionally interrupted their wanderings "from water hole to water hole over their almost desert country" to battle each other. They are not fighting for any apparent reason—for example, to obtain land or political power—but simply because fighting is part of their cultural tradition.

Warfare is "an invention," she concludes, like cooking, writing, or marriage. Once a society becomes exposed to the "idea" of war, then "they will sometimes go to war" under certain circumstances. Some societies, such as the Pueblo Indians, fight reluctantly to defend themselves against aggressors. Other peoples, such as the Plains Indians, would sally forth with enthusiasm, because they'd elevated martial skills to the highest of manly virtues; fighting bravely and well was the best way for a young man to achieve prestige and "win his sweetheart's smile of approval."

Mead's cultural model is simple and powerful. War, once invented, becomes a tradition, a custom, a habit, and its own cause. In the 1970s, the evolutionary biologist Richard Dawkins coined the term "meme" to describe religion and other self-perpetuating cultural beliefs and behaviors, which can sometimes spread in spite of the harm they do. Militarism—the culture of war—is a meme that can infect any society. Cultural, economic, and biological theories are not mutually exclusive; all these factors contribute to the emergence, spread, and persistence of war. But only Mead's explanation accounts for the puzzling fact that societies with no good reason to fight do so and others with every reason to fight don't.

Consider the case of the Waorani and the Semai, two tribal societies of hunter-farmers who live on different continents and whose behavior could not be more different. The Waorani dwell in the Ecuadorean Amazon, at the base of the Andes. When first observed by outsiders in the 1940s, the Waorani were widely dispersed and had food in abundance, and yet they incessantly raided each other's villages and those of neighboring tribes. Fights were initially triggered by accusations of witchcraft, disputes over women, and the theft of axes and other tools, but then violence became self-perpetuating. Warfare and homicide claimed as much as 60 percent of the population, almost double the casualty rate of the Yanomamö, making the Waorani one of the most violent tribal societies known to anthropology.

At the other end of the spectrum are the Semai, who live in the forests of Malaysia. The Semai population is sixty-eight times more dense (according to one estimate) than that of the Waorani, and they must work much harder to obtain food, because their soil is less fertile and game less plentiful. They are also much more prone than the Waorani to infections and other ailments. And yet the Semai are among the most peaceful tribal people ever studied. The Semai shun conflicts of any kind, verbal as well as physical. Men rarely if ever fight each other or beat their wives, nor do parents hit their children.

The Semai are not innate pacifists. That was demonstrated in the 1950s, when they were embroiled in a war between Malaysia's British rulers and communist guerrillas. After the communists killed some Semai men serving the British as scouts, other Semai sought vengeance. "We killed, killed, killed," one Semai man recalled. "Truly we were drunk with blood." After the war, however, the Semai veterans returned to their homes and peaceful ways. The anthropologists Clayton and Carole Robarchek, who did fieldwork among both the Waorani and the Semai, contend that their divergent behavior cannot be explained in terms of innate aggression or competition for resources, but only by deep-rooted, self-perpetuating cultural attitudes.

WHY WAR IS SO INFECTIOUS

Different cultures around the world—in Africa, Asia, Europe, Australia, and the New World—invented war independently, just as they independently invented cooking, stone tools, pottery, art, music, religion, agriculture, writing, and monumental architecture. War emerged among hunter-gatherers in Australia and California, among chiefdoms in the American northwest and in Polynesia, in the burgeoning states of the Mesopotamians, Egyptians, Indians, Chinese, Mayans, and Incas.

War was perhaps more likely to break out and persist in densely populated, circumscribed regions where people were dependent on agriculture, but these conditions were neither necessary nor sufficient. War erupted in different regions for different reasons: conflicts over food, land, water, mates, status, wealth, religion, power. Perhaps a squabble between two hunters over an antelope that both had speared escalated into a feud between their male relatives. Psychopaths might have started fights for the sheer thrill of it. But the custom of war persisted in the absence of these original causes, and it spread from one culture to another.

Why did the war meme spread so rapidly after its initial invention millennia ago? After all, unlike cooking, agriculture, and writing, which have obvious benefits, war is an extremely risky enterprise, which often inflicts harm on victors as well as losers. The answer to this riddle is that war, like an infectious disease, often spreads to societies that do not want it. If one tribe starts raiding its neighbors, the neighbors, even if they prefer to remain peaceful, have few options: submit, flee, fight, or resist nonviolently (an option to which I will return in chapter six).

Once begun, war often persists as each side seeks vengeance for past attacks. According to the anthropologist Lawrence Keeley, the desire for revenge was by far the most common motive of Native American warriors—ahead of the desire for land, booty, slaves, women, or prestige. Societies in a violent region also have a strong incentive to carry out preemptive attacks against potential attackers. The fear of war—like the fear of resource scarcity—breeds war, and so does war itself. Modern conflicts show the same epidemic-like pattern as prehistoric ones. One of the few clear-cut patterns uncovered by Lewis Fry Richardson, author of *Statistics of Deadly Quarrels*, was that war is "infectious," spreading from one region to another like a contagious disease.

War radically alters social relations in ways that perpetuate war, according to the anthropologist Sarah Blaffer Hrdy. She notes that for most of our evolutionary history, our hunter-gatherer forebears were egalitarian, with females and males enjoying roughly equal status. The emergence of war boosted the status of males, especially those who excelled at fighting, and diminished the position of women. Male dominance often led to other transformations, including sharper sexual divisions of labor, father-to-son inheritance of land and other assets, male fixation on female chastity, and even sequestration of women, including "walling off of boys beyond a certain age from intimate contact with women and children," Hrdy says. These patriarchal practices are "recipes for a society that values conquest over harmony."

Indeed, societies that had war thrust upon them made a virtue of necessity. They embraced all aspects of militarism and warfare; they honored their warriors, commemorated their exploits, granted them prestige and power. As Mead puts it, "The deeds of warriors are immortalized in the words of our poets; the toys of our children are modeled upon the weapons of war." War becomes an end in itself, at a basic level disconnected from any rational purpose.

THE VIRULENCE OF WESTERN WAR

Militarism not only spreads like a virus from society to society. It also becomes more virulent over time, as societies seek advantage over each other by inventing new weapons and tactics. Europeans brought their violent customs with them as they invaded the New World and other regions, just as they brought smallpox, syphilis, and other infectious diseases. Europeans attacked native people, forcing them to fight in self-defense. Europeans also introduced military practices and technologies—including horses and firearms—into these indigenous societies, which then waged war against each other and the invaders.

Native Americans waged war against each other long before Europeans arrived, but that does not mean they all fought all the time. In two momentous early encounters, Native Americans greeted Europeans with kindness and generosity. Here is how Christopher Columbus describes the Arawak, a tribal people living in the Bahamas when he landed there in 1492: "They... brought us parrots and balls of cotton and spears and many other things, which they exchanged for the glass beads and hawks' bells. They willingly traded everything they owned... They do not bear arms, and do not know them, for I showed them a sword, they took it by the edge and cut themselves out of ignorance... With fifty men we could subjugate them all and make them do whatever we want." Columbus was as good as his word. Within decades the Spaniards had enslaved or slaughtered almost all the Arawaks and other natives of the New Indies.

A milder version of this scenario unfolded in New England in the early seventeenth century. After the Pilgrims arrived in Plymouth in 1620, they almost starved to death. Members of a local tribe, the Wampanoag, helped the newcomers, showing them how to plant corn and other local foods. In the fall of 1621, the Pilgrims celebrated their first successful harvest with a three-day feast with the Wampanoag. The kindness of the Wampanoag was striking, because they had recently been ravaged by diseases caught from previous European explorers. Europeans had also killed, kidnapped, and enslaved Native Americans in the region. As English settlers poured in and seized more and more land from the Wampanoag and other tribes, the natives eventually did resist with violence, in vain. This same pattern recurred throughout the New World over the next two centuries, leading to the virtual annihilation of Native Americans.

The historian John Keegan traces the western style of war back to the win-at-all-costs philosophy of ancient Sparta. This ruthless attitude, he suggests, combined with increasingly deadly tactics and weaponry, helped European states gain control over much of the world. Western powers also turned on each other, with increasingly catastrophic consequences. Keegan once confessed that after decades of pondering World War I, he was more baffled than ever as to why it happened. World War I "terminated European dominance of the world and, through the suffering it inflicted on the participant populations, corrupted what was best in their civilization—its liberalism and hopefulness," he writes in *A History of Warfare*. World War II "completed the ruin."

Keegan rejects the famous dictum of the Prussian statesman Carl von Clausewitz that "war is the continuation of policy by other means." The implication of this aphorism is that war is a rational social endeavor; states and other organizations wage wars as a means to an end, such as security and prosperity. The cataclysmic conflicts of the modern era, Keegan asserts, show how war can become an end in itself, pursued well past any sensible benefits for states, leaders, or citizens. War's absurdity is embodied in humanity's deadliest invention, nuclear weapons, which threaten not only their creators but also all life on Earth. Keegan, like Mead, views war as a cultural phenomenon. War, he asserts, stems primarily not from human nature, poverty, or religious and ethnic divisions but from the "institution of war itself."

DOCILITY AND WAR CRIMES

To call war cultural is not to deny that biology contributes to its propagation. Far from it. The war meme resembles a wily con artist tailoring his con to exploit victims' vulnerabilities, whether greed or compassion. War, similarly, can tap into fear, aggression, ambition, and desire for vengeance—our negative traits—as well as ostensibly good ones such as empathy and altruism. The altruism of primates—manifested when a female chimpanzee jumps into a moat to rescue a drowning adolescent—gives the primatologist Frans de Waal hope that humanity can overcome its darker impulses. But he acknowledges that our affection for members of our in-group—whether family, troop, village, nation, race, or religion—sometimes translates into hostility toward "others." Soldier ants act altruistically when they attack ants from another nest, or chimps when they ambush a member of a rival troop.

A human soldier demonstrates altruism when he charges an enemy machine gun pinning down his buddies, as does a suicide bomber who flies a plane into a skyscraper in the name of his fundamentalist sect. These acts of lethal self-sacrifice are so extreme that they are hard to explain in terms of conventional Darwinian theory. In a 1990 paper in *Science*, the Nobel-winning economist and cognitive scientist Herbert Simon speculates that extreme altruism stems from innate "docility," or "receptivity to social influence." We are social creatures, he explains, and so natural selection bred a certain degree of docility into our ancestors. Those who go along, as the old saying goes, *get al*ong, and those who defy the social order may find themselves ostracized or worse.

Simon points out that leaders of a hierarchical society can exploit their subjects' docility by urging or coercing them to do things that don't benefit the subjects but do benefit the leaders. Our susceptibility to leaders' exhortations is compounded by what Simon calls our "bounded rationality," which sometimes keeps us from calculating what is really in our best interests. Simon's theory makes all too much sense. Docility and bounded rationality—or stupidity, to put it more bluntly—help explain why young men throughout history have embraced the terrible lie of the Roman propagandist Horace: *dulce et decorum est pro patria mori.* "It is sweet and honorable to die for one's country."

Docility can also explain why ordinary people can commit acts of extraordinary cruelty. Yale psychologist Stanley Milgram devised an experiment in the 1960s in response to the Holocaust, which left him pondering the mind-set of the Nazis. In Milgram's experiments, subjects are told that they are participating in a test of another person's learning ability. The subject reads pairs of words to the "learner"—who is in an adjoining room and can be heard but not seen by the subject—and then tests his ability to remember the pairings. Each time the learner fails to remember a pairing, the scientist, who is in the same room as the subject, orders him to give the learner a stronger electric shock. As the shocks increase, the learner reacts with audible distress, crying out in pain, banging on the wall, and even claiming that he is about to have a heart attack. After a certain point, the learner falls silent.

In reality, the learner is an actor pretending to be shocked. If the subject hesitates to deliver stronger shocks, the scientist insists that he continue, adding that the subject will not be held responsible for anything that happens to the learner. Only if the subject resists four successive commands from the scientist is the experiment stopped. Otherwise the experiment continues until the subject administers a "shock" of 450 volts to the learner. (Electrical outlets in the U.S. usually deliver 120 volts.)

Before the experiment, Milgram asked forty psychiatrists to predict the results; the average guess was that only 1 percent of the subjects, those with psychopathic, sadistic tendencies, would deliver the strongest shock. But in Milgram's initial experiment twenty-six out of forty subjects, or around two thirds, administered what they believed to be the strongest, life-threatening shock. Many of the subjects expressed concern for the learner, but their docility overrode their empathy. Versions of Milgram's experiment have been repeated in the U.S. and elsewhere with similar results.

In a 1973 article in *Harper's Magazine*, Milgram spells out the implications of his research: "The extreme willingness of adults to go to almost any lengths on the command of an authority constitutes the chief finding of the study and the fact most urgently demanding explanation... Ordinary people, simply doing their jobs, and without any particular hostility on their part, can become agents in a terrible destructive process." Milgram calls our deference to authority "a fatal flaw," which "in the long run gives our species only a modest chance for survival." His experiment places the debate over whether violent aggression is learned or innate in a new light. We often act viciously out of innate docility, not innate aggression. We kill and torture because we're sheep, not psychopathic wolves.

THE BAD BARRELS PROBLEM

Another disturbing demonstration of the power of culture to shape our behavior—and to shut down our innate empathy toward others—is the Stanford Prison Experiment, carried out in 1971 by the psychologist Philip Zimbardo. The experiment demonstrates how readily, and arbitrarily, we separate people into "us" and "them"—that is, those who are part of our group and hence deserving of our empathy versus those who are not.

For the experiment, Zimbardo created a mock prison in which twenty-four Stanford students played the role of prisoners and guards. He screened the students for mental stability and assigned their roles randomly. Guards and prisoners alike were white, middle-class males at one of the top schools in the country, and yet they quickly adopted adversarial roles. One key factor was that guards dressed in khaki uniforms and wore sunglasses to prevent eye contact. Prisoners wore smocks, and were referred to by numbers instead of their names.

Guards were not allowed to strike prisoners. But within two days, some guards had become abusive, screaming at prisoners, yanking mattresses from their cells, denying them food, and not allowing them to empty buckets into which they urinated and defecated. Some prisoners protested, and five quit the experiment, but others passively accepted their treatment and even helped guards punish other prisoners. After six days, Zimbardo's horrified girlfriend (and later wife) convinced him to end the experiment, which had been scheduled to run for two weeks.

In 2004, the Stanford Prison Experiment suddenly seemed more relevant than ever, after the media released photographs revealing that American soldiers had abused Iraqis held at Abu Ghraib prison. Some of the soldiers' abuse—which included forcing prisoners to strip and to engage in simulated homosexual intercourse—was strikingly similar to acts perpetrated by "guards" in the Stanford Prison Experiment. Reacting to the Abu Ghraib coverage, Secretary of Defense Donald Rumsfeld and other military leaders blamed the abuse on a few "rogue" or "rotten" soldiers. Read: bad apples. Eleven of the guards were court-martialed.

Zimbardo, who served as an expert witness at the trial of one of the Abu Ghraib guards, disputes Rumsfeld's explanation. In his 2007 book *The Lucifer Effect*, Zimbardo argues that the histories of the guards at Abu Ghraib reveal no psychopathy or other disorders. The guards behaved badly not because they were bad apples, Zimbardo says, but because they were in a "bad barrel," a situation that encouraged brutality toward Iraqi prisoners. Human aggression and cruelty stem less from the "disposition" of individuals than from their environment, or "situation," Zimbardo proposes. Studies of modern suicide bombers, torturers, and war criminals, he notes, reveal many to be—as Hannah Arendt said of the Nazi war criminals— "terrifyingly normal."

In war, a soldier's eagerness to please his leaders—and protect and avenge his comrades—can turn him into a monster. In 1968, 105 American soldiers in Charlie Company entered the tiny

Vietnamese village of My Lai. Within a few hours, the soldiers had shot, bayoneted, and blown up 500 unarmed villagers, almost all of them women, children, infants, and elderly men. The soldiers slaughtered all the animals in the village too. Some soldiers sodomized and sexually mutilated women before killing them.

Lieutenant William Calley, the company leader, who was convicted of 104 counts of murder, was by all accounts not a sadistic psychopath but a mild-mannered, soft-spoken, religious man. He insisted that he was following his commanding officer's order to "destroy" the village. In his autobiography, Calley also cites a biblical precedent for Charlie Company's slaughter of men, women, children, and even animals. In the Book of Samuel, God commands Saul, King of the Israelites, to destroy a rival society, the Amalekites. More specifically, God orders Saul "to spare them not; but slay both man and woman, infant and suckling, ox and sheep, camel and ass." When Calley ordered his men to kill babies and cows, he saw himself as a good man deferring to the highest of all authorities.

Atrocities like My Lai, Zimbardo points out, are all too probable consequences of war. "Under the extreme stress of combat conditions, with fatigue, fear, anger, hatred, and revenge at full throttle, men can lose their moral compass," he writes. "Then the furies are released in unimaginable orgies of rape and murder of civilians as well as enemy soldiers." War is the ultimate bad barrel.

IS OUR ERA LIKE 1910?

Biological pessimists fear war is so innate that we may never abolish it. Freud is succumbing to biological pessimism when he worries that humanity might be destroyed by its "death instinct." Some scholars who view war as driven primarily by culture rather than biology are equally gloomy about the prospects for permanent peace. Call them cultural pessimists. Stanley Milgram was a cultural pessimist. So is Zimbardo, who was Milgram's classmate at a New York City high school. When I asked him in an interview if war will ever end, he shook his head grimly. Wars, he replied, can at best only be reduced and never entirely abolished. It is just too easy for unscrupulous leaders to manipulate followers into hating and hurting "others."

Another cultural pessimist is the journalist Barbara Ehrenreich. In her 1996 book *Blood Rites*, she describes war as "one of the 'fittest' of memes," because it thrives not just in authoritarian, patriarchal cultures but even in liberal democratic ones like the United States. Wars "produce warlike societies," she writes, "which, in turn, make the world more dangerous for other societies, which are thus recruited into being more warlike themselves." Those trying to eradicate the meme of militarism, she warns, "must prepare themselves to lose battle after battle and still fight on, to lose security, comfort, position, even life."

In May 2010, I got an especially bracing dose of pessimism at a conference at Ohio State University called "Hybrid Warfare: The Struggle of Military Forces to Adapt to Complex Opponents from the Ancient World to the Present." "Hybrid warfare" is military jargon for conflicts involving both uniformed, state-sponsored armies and "unconventional" forces, variously termed irregulars, guerrillas, militias, insurgents, revolutionaries, terrorists, or resistance fighters. With one exception, all the speakers were military historians, and some were soldiers as well as scholars.

The historians did not question whether past wars were just in their cause or conduct, or should have been waged in the first place. Rather, they sought practical lessons that could help the U.S. and its allies prevail in future wars. Some speakers warned that a major power could win battles but lose wars with ruthless tactics, which can stiffen the resolve of the enemy and transform neutral civilians into combatants. Others noted that brutality can be quite effective in certain situations. General Sherman's destruction of Atlanta and other cities during the U.S. Civil War certainly "worked," one scholar pointed out.

The implicit assumption of the conference was that there will always be wars of one kind or another. This view was confirmed for me by the meeting's organizer, Peter Mansoor, who teaches military history at Ohio State and has written books about World War II and the war in Iraq. With his close-cropped hair, square jaw, and no-nonsense demeanor, Mansoor looks and speaks like a soldier, and he was one. After graduating from West Point in 1982, he served in the Army for twenty-six years, rising to the level of colonel. He commanded the 1st Brigade, 1st Armored Division in Iraq from 2003 to 2005, and later served as executive officer to General David Petraeus when he commanded U.S. forces in Iraq.

When I asked if humanity will ever renounce militarism and war, Mansoor replied with an immediate, head-shaking "no." "I don't think there's anything that could convince me that major war or even another world war couldn't happen in the future," he said. Mansoor was unimpressed by the absence of war between major powers over the past few decades. He likened our era to the relative calm in Europe following the end of the Napoleonic wars in 1815.

"You had a long period of stability, punctuated by some regional conflicts—the Crimean War, the Franco–Prussian War—but nothing that drew the entire continent into a massive conflict." By the early twentieth century, he noted, some prominent intellectuals proposed that the growing economic interdependence of European powers made war between them unlikely. "World War I and World War II show that obviously wasn't the case," Mansoor says. "We could be in this long period of stability in the wake of the end of the cold war, where there are regional conflicts, little brushfire wars, as we're seeing in Iraq and Afghanistan." The U.S. must remain prepared to wage war against not only rogue states, insurgencies, and terrorist groups, he said, but also major powers, including those possessing nuclear weapons. Nuclear weapons provide a deterrent, but not "insurance against great-power war breaking out. I just think it means that if it does break out, it would be a lot more deadly than what we've seen in the past."

Equally pessimistic was the sole non-historian who spoke at the conference, a four-star Marine Corp general named James Mattis. Like Mansoor, Mattis believes that war is eternal, because civilized democracies like the U.S. will always have enemies, whether Nazis or Islamic fundamentalists. "The enemy is going to continue to be there, the enemy of what I call the values of the Enlightenment," Mattis said. "The nature of man has not changed, unfortunately. And it's not going to change any time soon, I don't think. So we are going to have to be ready to fight, across the range of military operations, whatever the enemy chooses to do."

Mattis apparently subscribes to the "bad apple" theory of war, which holds that even if most of us want peace, incorrigibly violent, aggressive people will keep dragging us back into war. Two months after the Ohio meeting, Barack Obama— who, you might recall, has declared that "we will not eradicate violent conflict in our lifetime"—put Mattis in charge of U.S. Central Command, with oversight of the U.S. wars in Afghanistan and Iraq. Pessimism pervades the foreign policy of the most powerful nation on Earth.

CENSORSHIP AND OTHER CULTURAL SOLUTIONS

Some visionaries have advocated radical cultural solutions to eradicate the contagion of war once and for all. Religions can all be seen as schemes for ending lethal conflict. All the world's great religions, in principle, encourage us to behave altruistically toward others, but in practice they often provoke lethal intolerance.

A popular secular solution calls for nations to disarm and yield their sovereignty to a global government, which would resolve international disputes. The anthropologist Robert Carneiro suggests that a "world state" would represent the natural culmination of the integration of our species into larger and larger social units, which began some ten thousand years ago. Bertrand Russell and Albert Einstein, among other anti-war activists, advocated the global government solution.

Leaving aside questions of feasibility, some peace activists fear that the global government solution might quickly become a problem. "If we had a world government," the Nobel-winning chemist and peace activist Linus Pauling once told me, "Hitler reincarnated might gain control over it. And in any case the power elite would no doubt strive to get control over it, just as they have over the United States." Other activists, such as the journalist Bill McKibben, insist that we should go in the opposite direction toward small, decentralized government—which I worry might leave us more vulnerable to attacks from violent groups.

Would eliminating weapons eliminate war? Arms-control treaties have undoubtedly helped make the world safer. Successful treaties include the 1963 ban on aboveground nuclear tests, which had been blanketing the planet in radioactive fallout; the 1972 ban on biological weapons; the 1993 ban on chemical weapons; and the 1999 ban on land mines. The U.S. and Russia have also negotiated cuts in their nuclear arsenals since the end of the cold war.

But the correlation between arms possession and violence is not as strong as one might think. During the Rwandan genocide in the early 1990s, Hutus slaughtered hundreds of thousands of Tutsis with machetes and clubs. The Swiss, who issue rifles and train in their use as part of the country's civil defense program, rank behind only Americans and Yemenis in per capita firearms ownership, and yet they are among the world's least violent people. In other words, people don't kill simply because they have the means to do so, and if they want to kill each other, they will find a way.

Dave Grossman, the retired Army colonel whose research on the psychology of combat I discuss in chapter two, advocates restrictions on the sale and consumption of films, television shows, and video games that depict war and other forms of violence as exciting, which of course includes a huge proportion of the entertainment industry. Violent media, and especially extremely realistic "first-person shooter" games, condition users to overcome their natural aversion to killing, Grossman contends, and hence make them more likely to become mass murderers or war criminals.

I'm a staunch defender of freedom of all forms of speech. So I would be loathe to support censorship of the media even if research turned up evidence for Grossman's claim that violent entertainment is provoking an epidemic of real violence, including war. But a few basic statistics contradict his claim. In 1991, the U.S. homicide rate peaked at 9.8 for every 100,000 people. This was the highest rate since 1933, the violent final year of Prohibition. Since then, homicides have fallen by almost one half. Some criminologists attribute this drop in part to increased incarceration, but recently incarceration rates have fallen, too. Meanwhile, over the past two decades consumption of violent games, films, television shows, and internet videos has surged in the U.S. as well as Japan, Canada, Europe, and other affluent regions, which have rates of homicide much lower than that of the U.S. War-related casualties have also declined during this period.

The political scientist J. David Singer saw war as far too complex for any single solution. Singer founded the Correlates of War project, one of the largest databases on modern armed conflict. I first spoke to Singer about his research in 1991, and we talked on and off until his death in 2009. Like Lewis Fry Richardson, the author of *Statistics of Deadly Quarrels*, Singer spent his career studying war to find ways to prevent it, and like Richardson he never really found an answer.

Singer's research, for the most part, undercut proposed solutions for war, especially hawkish ones. He found no evidence for the claim that the best way to keep the peace is to prepare for war (that is, to maintain a powerful military). Nor did he turn up support for the notion that aggression, if unchecked, leads to more aggression, or that alliances can help maintain peace. Allies, although less likely to fight each other, are more likely to fight overall than non-allied nations.

Like Richardson's analysis, Singer's suggests that wars break out at random, without conforming to any laws or patterns. Singer concludes that we are "softwired" for war. The problem, he writes, is not our innate aggression so much as our propensity for deferring to authority and embracing our culture's values, including militaristic ones. Singer was not immune to these influences. In an essay, he recalls being "very disappointed" that World War II ended just before he completed his training as a naval officer. He worries that "cultural evolution is nearly as resistant to change as genetic evolution."

UNINVENTING WAR

Margaret Mead was hardly the naïve optimist that her detractors have accused her of being. In "Warfare Is Only an Invention" she asks: "If we know that it is not inevitable, that it is due to historical accident that warfare is one of the ways in which we think of behaving, are we given any hope by that?" Not necessarily, she continues, because once an invention is known and accepted, men do not easily relinquish it. Writing at the dawn of World War II, Mead had good reason to fear that militarism has become too deeply embedded in modern culture to eradicate.

Mead argues that for an invention to become obsolete, "people must recognize the defects of the old invention, and someone must make a new one." In this way, trial by jury supplanted trial by ordeal or combat, which had come to seem "unfair, capricious, alien." She adds that "to invent forms of behavior which will make war obsolete, it is a first requirement to believe that such an invention is possible." In other words, if we're sure war will never end, our belief may be self-fulfilling.

Some societies may be so "addicted" to war—as Chris Hedges warns in *War Is a Force That Gives Us Meaning*—that they may not *want* peace. In her 1935 book *Sex and Temperament in Three Primitive Societies*, Mead describes a tribal people in New Guinea, the Mundugumor, who were enthusiastic practitioners of war and cannibalism. They abandoned these customs reluctantly, only after Australian authorities threatened tribal leaders with imprisonment. Mead calls our malleability and conformity a "two-edged sword"; in principle, we have the freedom to create whatever society we choose, but we may also fall under the spell of pathological cultural norms. History confirms this dark truth. Over and over, warmongering leaders have exploited the docility, bounded rationality, and altruism of their subjects and manipulated them into hating and attacking outsiders, and even each other.

On the other hand, good leaders can help us recognize our commonality with others and appreciate the advantages of peace. Many of history's most admired figures—Buddha, Jesus, Martin Luther King, Gandhi, and Mead herself—have attempted to do just that. And rather than exploiting our docility, stupidity, and suspicion of those who seem unlike us, these preachers of peace are appealing to our intelligence, empathy, and even self-interest—and our ability to take control of our own destinies.

We will only relinquish the invention of war, Mead proposes, if we find another invention to replace it. I disagree with Mead on this point. As the anthropologist Douglas Fry documents in his book *The Human Potential for Peace*, humans have already invented countless methods for resolving disputes nonviolently, some of which predate the invention of states. The Hopi settled arguments with shoving contests, and the Mehinaku of Brazil with wrestling matches. The Netsilik, an Inuit people, engaged in "song duels" consisting mostly of comical insults. Among Australian Aborigines, one man might seek to defuse hostility between others with clownish antics and jokes.

The Semai convened meetings called *berharaa*, in which disputants, their relatives, and any other interested villagers gathered in the house of a headman. The meeting could last for days, during which the dispute was explored from every possible perspective, before the headman finally offered his opinion on the matter and emphasized the need for harmony. In the seventeenth century a half dozen tribes in the American northeast, tired of fighting each other, formed what came to be called the Iroquois Confederacy. A kind of precursor of the

United Nations, it called for tribal representatives to meet to discuss disputes and negotiate agreements.

Modern societies resolve conflicts via a wide range of institutions, from local courts to town halls to senates to parliaments and all the way up to the World Court and the United Nations. Humans "have a great capacity for dealing with conflicts nonviolently," Fry writes. We have the ways to end war. We need only the will. As the next chapter shows, some extremely belligerent societies have found the will, and there are even tantalizing signs that humanity as a whole may be choosing peace.

CHAPTER FIVE

Choosing Peace

As a boy growing up in Turkey in the early twentieth century, Muzafer Sherif had first hand knowledge of war's horror. In 1919, he barely survived a massacre carried out by Greek soldiers in his hometown, Smyrna. After emigrating to America, Sherif earned a doctorate as a social psychologist and started exploring, among other topics, our tendency to separate people into "us" and "them." He is remembered today primarily for the Robbers Cave Experiment, which he carried out in 1954. Like the studies of Milgram and Zimbardo, Sherif's has become a classic of social science research, but it has a much happier ending.

Sherif brought twenty-two fifth-grade boys to a camp at Robbers Cave State Park in Oklahoma and divided them into two groups, Rattlers and Eagles. Sherif housed the boys in separate cabins and kept them apart for a week, during which boys in each group bonded and grew suspicious of the "others" whom they could only see and hear at a distance. Sherif finally brought the Rattlers and Eagles together and pitted them against each other in swimming races, tugs-of-war, and other competitions.

Rattlers and Eagles were soon hurling insults at each other, like "tubby," "fatso," "sissy," "baby," "communist," and "little black Sambo" (even though all the boys were white). The boys also started "brutalizing and raiding each other with sticks, bats, and rocks in socks," the psychologist Steven Pinker notes in his best seller *How the Mind Works*. Pinker cites the Sherif experiment as evidence of how readily we can be manipulated into hating and fighting others. "Jingoism is alarmingly easy to evoke," he writes, "even without a scarce resource to fight over."

But Pinker neglects to mention the second half of the experiment, during which Sherif presented the Rattlers and Eagles with "problems" that they could solve only by cooperating. Sherif told the boys that the camp could rent a movie, *Treasure Island*, only if all the boys chipped in money, which they did. Then a camp truck "broke down," and all the boys had to push it to jump-start it. Another pseudo-malfunction forced the Rattlers and Eagles to share a truck on an outing. The hostility between the Rattlers and Eagles soon dissolved and they became friends, laughingly recalling their previous exploits against each other. On the last day at Robbers Cave, they voted to take the same bus home.

So yes, we all too readily separate people into those like "us," whom we treat empathetically and altruistically, versus those we treat as "others." Leaders can exploit this tendency to drum up support for persecution, repression, war, and genocide. But we can clearly also learn to overcome our hostility toward others, and not just because we have been manipulated into doing so, like the boys at Robbers Cave. We can use our reason to recognize our commonality with others, or at the very least to resolve our differences nonviolently.

Sherif extracted another optimistic lesson from his experiment. In a 1958 paper, he proposes that traditionally hostile groups can overcome their differences if they are bound together by "superordinate," or shared, goals. We have many such goals today, but two stand out. One is figuring out how we can all prosper in every sense—materially as well as spiritually—without irrevocably damaging our planet. Another, which will help us achieve the first, is ending war.

RELINQUISHING WAR

Throughout history, people in a wide range of societies, some of which were once quite bellicose, have renounced war, at least temporarily. One notable warrior-turned-pacifist was the legendary Indian emperor Ashoka, who lived in the third century BCE During the first part of his rule, he unified all of India through brutal wars and repression. He was ruthless, even killing his brothers to eliminate them as rivals. But after an especially bloody war against a rebellious province, Ashoka embraced Buddhism and its doctrine of ahimsa, or nonviolence, and he renounced war, executions of criminals, and even the slaughter of animals.

What we know of Ashoka derives mostly from ancient stone inscriptions that probably mix myth with fact. But modern history offers well-documented examples of societies relinquishing war. The Vikings were once the scourge of Europe, raiding lands

as far away as modern-day Iraq. Their Swedish descendants created an empire via wars of conquest against Poland, Russia, and
other northern European states. The Swedes' last armed conflict
took place in 1814, when they forcibly annexed Norway. Like-
wise, the Swiss were once famed as mercenaries. The Vatican's
Swiss Guard is a relic of this martial past. But like Sweden, Switzerland has remained neutral since the Napoleonic wars.

In 1948, Costa Rica's corrupt legislature refused to turn
over power to a newly elected president. An armed uprising
led by businessman-turned-revolutionary José Figueres overthrew the government in a battle that killed more than two
thousand people in forty-four days. The new regime rewrote
the national constitution, granting voting rights to women and
blacks and abolishing the army, which previous governments
had employed to repress political opposition. Costa Rica has
remained disarmed and peaceful ever since, while violence
(often exacerbated by U.S. policies in the region) has wracked
Nicaragua, Honduras, Panama, Guatemala, El Salvador, and
other nations in Central America.

I don't want to overstate the pacifism of these societies.
Ashoka, the Buddhist emperor, never entirely abolished his
army. Costa Rica could take the risk of disarming in part
because it aligned itself with the U.S. during the cold war and
cut off ties with Cuba after its communist revolution. Sweden
and Switzerland traded with Germany during World Wars
I and II, in part to keep it at bay. Both countries maintain
armed forces for self-defense and have contributed troops to
international peacekeeping operations. But if all nations emu-
lated these nations, there would be no war.

One of my favorite examples of people turning away from war are the Waorani. As I mentioned in the previous chapter, this Amazonian tribe had a rate of violent death twice as high as that of the "fierce" Yanomamö. When contacted by anthropologists in the 1950s, some Waorani deplored the savagery of their inter-village raiding, which they realized threatened them with extinction. But their intense distrust and hostility dissuaded rivals from meeting to hash out a truce, and they felt they had no choice but to keep fighting. "Warfare, under these conditions, is contagious," the anthropologists Clayton and Carole Robarchek point out. "Once one group adopts it as a tactic for advancing its ends, others must take it up or be destroyed."

Then several Waorani women who had fled the carnage and lived with other tribes returned to their village, accompanied by two American missionaries, and they came up with a plan to end the epidemic of violence. Using a small plane, the missionaries flew Waorani from hostile bands over each other's camps so that they could deliver conciliatory messages over a loudspeaker. These contacts were followed by face-to-face meetings. The first encounter went badly; a Waorani band from one village killed the emissary from another. But within a few months the inter-group raids ceased, and the Waorani soon reaped further benefits as they began trading and inter-marrying. Peace, it seems, can be contagious too.

The Waorani, far from missing the constant combat, "unanimously stressed their relief that the cycle of killing has come to an end," recall the Robarcheks. They emphasize that the Waorani relinquished war without any other dramatic changes in their situation. They did not all convert to Christianity. Nor were they conquered and disarmed by an outside force. They did not overhaul their social or sexual relationships or their methods for obtaining and distributing food. The main reason why war among the Waorani ended, the Robarcheks say, is because "the people themselves made a conscious decision to end it."

WAR VERSUS SLAVERY

The crucial first step toward peace is for people to reject war. To say, "Enough!" The political scientist and anti-war activist Randall Forsberg arrived at this conclusion late in her career, after decades of pursuing peace through arms control agreements. In the early 1980s, she spearheaded the nuclear freeze movement, which called for a moratorium on testing and deployment of new nuclear weapons by the U.S. and Soviet Union. During the summer of 1982, a coalition of peace groups, which I joined as a volunteer, organized a nuclear freeze rally in New York City's Central Park attended by as many as 1 million people.

The freeze referendum failed to win sufficient popular support to slow down the Reagan administration's buildup of nuclear weapons. Forsberg, undeterred, came up with an even more ambitious program for disarmament. In a 1999 paper, she proposed that all nations reduce arms to minimal levels, needed only for self-defense. Nations would resolve disputes before an "International Court of Justice," the decisions of which would be binding. Just as the freeze campaign had no real hope of success during the Reagan administration, so Forsberg's proposal for international disarmament was ignored after 9/11.

When I interviewed Forsberg in 2003, she no longer viewed arms and armies as the chief impediment to peace. Instead, her focus had switched to cultural—and especially moral—attitudes toward war. For as long as she could remember, she had had an aversion to war; that's why she became obsessed with ending it. She did not merely view war as irrational and immoral. She was repulsed by it. "The idea that people settle political disputes by blowing up bodies..." Forsberg paused and grimaced, as if overcome by a foul odor. "It's just unthinkable! Barbaric in the most primitive sense."

She always assumed that most people shared her view, but she gradually realized that many rational, decent citizens, scholars, and leaders—including some of her colleagues in the arms control community—still saw war as a legitimate form of resolving disputes in certain circumstances. This cultural tolerance of war, Forsberg claimed, accounts for its persistence, and not "innate aggressive impulses." To end war, Forsberg concluded, we need a "change in moral beliefs, not a change in power or politics."

She noted that shifts in moral attitudes led to the eradication—or at least outlawing in most societies—of once sanctioned practices such as cannibalism, human sacrifice, corporal punishment, and slavery. Like war, these bad habits arose thousands of years ago, primarily in agrarian societies, and some of them—notably slavery—remained legal and socially accepted, even in supposedly "civilized" societies, well into the nineteenth century.

Proponents of slavery cited biblical scripture and, later, pseudo-scientific theories to make the case that these practices were "natural" and hence inevitable. Most nations have none-theless abolished slavery, cannibalism, human sacrifice, and corporal punishment out of growing "respect for the dignity and worth of every individual," Forsberg once wrote. War will surely be next. "If we got to the point of thinking about war as being as gross and inhumanly awful as cannibalism," she told me, "then war would never come back."

I agree with Forsberg that the abolition of war would be a natural consequence of our growing recognition of human rights. This recognition has inspired a host of social transformations in addition to the ones Forsberg specifies, including legal protections for women, workers, children, ethnic and religious minorities, and homosexuals. On the other hand, we shouldn't congratulate ourselves too much on our moral enlightenment. Lincoln's Emancipation Proclamation of 1863 initially freed slaves in rebel regions but not in loyal ones, and it was at least in part a political and even military stratagem aimed at the south. The U.S. passed child labor laws during the Great Depression to preserve precious jobs for adults. Today, the U.S. and other supposed paragons of justice often pay lip service to individual dignity while still permitting discrimination, economic exploitation, and other abusive practices at home and abroad. Slavery, while not legally sanctioned, persists belowground. Seen in this context, war's persistence seems a bit less anomalous.

There are also crucial differences between war and the other cruel customs on which Forsberg focuses. One society can unilaterally ban slavery, human sacrifice, burning at the stake, and cannibalism without regard for the behavior of neighboring societies. If one society disarms, however, it becomes vulnerable to attacks from others. And you can't stop slavery with more slavery, or cannibalism with cannibalism, but you can stop armed aggression with armed aggression. Allied opposition to Imperial Japan and Nazi Germany forced them to relinquish their warlike ways.

Even pacifists must acknowledge that some wars have had better outcomes—and have been more legitimate—than others. War is thus more morally complex than, say, slavery, to which it is often compared. I don't consider my father and grandfather to be the ethical equivalents of slave-owners because they fought in World War II. I'm proud of them. The terrible, tragic irony is that every relatively "successful" war—and especially World War II, the deadliest conflict of all time—helps perpetuate war's legitimacy, making future wars more likely.

Forsberg, who died in 2007, was well aware of these paradoxical aspects of war. Although she loathed war, she was not a pacifist—"because of Hitler." She was nonetheless confident that war would one day fade away, just as other inhumane customs have. In fact, she saw signs of a growing revulsion toward war not only in massive protests against the U.S. invasion of Iraq in 2003, but also in the decline of major international wars since World War II. War, she said, "is on the wane."

THE DECLINE OF WAR

War "on the wane"? At first glance, this claim might seem absurd. My favorite source of data on military matters is the Stockholm International Peace Research Institute. According to the *SIPRI Yearbook 2011*, major armed conflicts—which by definition include at least one government-sponsored force and kill at least one thousand people a year—wrack fifteen regions in Asia, Africa, the Americas, and the Middle East. These regions include Rwanda, Somalia, Sudan, Colombia, Peru, Kashmir, Myanmar, the Philippines, and Kurdistan. SIPRI's list does not include Libya and other Arab nations where civil conflicts erupted in 2011.

Between 2001 and 2011, global military spending surged more than 50 percent. U.S. outlays grew by 81 percent to $698 billion, which is almost as much as the rest of the world combined. The next biggest military spender after the U.S. is China at $119 billion a year. Humanity is awash in weapons, from AK-47s to nuclear-tipped missiles. The eight declared nuclear powers possess an estimated 20,530 warheads. For many people around the world, war provides not just meaning, excitement, and political power but also enormous profits.

But other data lend support to the idea that we are losing our taste for war. Estimating war casualties, including civilians, has always been extremely difficult. War zones are not exactly conducive to things like counting bodies. Scholars also debate what counts as a casualty, or a war. Should only wars between states count? Civil wars? Colonial uprisings against imperial powers? Genocidal campaigns? Deaths from famine and disease in war zones as well as from bombs and bullets? Bias is rampant among estimators. Combatants, government representatives, U.N. officials, journalists, anti-war and human-rights groups, medical organizations, and scholars have different national, religious, ethnic, and ideological allegiances, which sometimes motivate them to inflate or deflate numbers.

Not surprisingly, body counts often diverge wildly. Estimates of World War I deaths range from under 8 million to over 17 million (the higher number includes civilian deaths). Counts of the civilians killed in Iraq between 2003 and 2006 range from 48,000 to 600,000. All casualty statistics—especially those with pretensions of precision—should be taken with large grains of salt. But investigations by a wide variety of groups reveal a dramatic, recent drop in the worldwide incidence and lethality of war.

The twentieth century produced the greatest carnage in human history, at least measured in absolute (rather than proportional) terms. The political scientist Rudolph Rummel distinguishes war from "democide," his term for mass slaughter of civilians by their own governments, which accounted for far more bloodshed than international or civil wars. (Unlike genocide, which is directed at certain ethnic or religious groups, democide involves killing any civilians.) Rummel estimates that democide—which includes deaths from famine and disease as well as violence—killed 262 million people between 1900 and 1999 and war another forty-three million for a total of 305 million. He contends, for example, that Mao's Great Leap Forward resulted in the death by starvation of thirty-eight million people between 1958 and 1962.

The political scientist Milton Leitenberg proposes a lower number of deaths, 241 million, for the twentieth century. Of this total, 190 million deaths occurred between 1900 and 1945 and another 41 million between 1945 and 2000. According to these statistics, which include direct and indirect deaths, the toll from war dropped from about 4 million a year in the first half of the twentieth century to less than 1 million in the second half. During this same period, the world's population more than doubled.

The decline has become even more dramatic since 2000. One organization that tracks war casualties is the Geneva Declaration on Armed Violence and Development. This U.N.-affiliated organization, which is based in Switzerland and sponsored by more than ninety states (not including the U.S.), is committed to achieving "measurable reductions in the global burden of armed violence." In 2008, the Geneva Declaration issued a report, "Global Burden of Armed Violence," which notes that since 2000 annual war-related deaths have fallen well below rates in the twentieth century.

"Wars grab headlines, but the individual risk of dying violently in an armed conflict is today relatively low," the report states. Drawing upon several different studies, the report estimates that between 2004 and 2007, an average of 52,000 soldiers and civilians died violently each year in armed conflicts, including civil wars and terrorism. If deaths from "indirect" war-related causes such as disease and famine are included, the average annual total rises to 250,000. Almost twice as many people, 490,000, are homicide victims, and more than three times as many, 800,000, are suicides.

On December 2, 2010, the Human Security Report Project, which is based at Simon Fraser University in Canada and sponsored by Norway, Sweden, Switzerland, England, and Canada, issued another encouraging report. It notes that the global economic downturn, which started in 2008, "did not lead to the expected increase in political violence" (again, contradicting the linkage of scarcity to conflict). Deaths of combatants in wars crept up a bit between 2005 and 2008 but are still quite low compared to averages in the twentieth century; moreover, in 2008 "the estimated number of civilians killed by organized violence was the lowest since data started being collected in 1989." The Simon Fraser researchers attribute this decline in part to immunizations and other healthcare measures that have reduced infant and child mortality rates in war zones.

The decline in war-related mortality over the past two decades corresponds to a decline in "high-intensity" wars, which kill at least one thousand people a year, the Simon Fraser group asserts. There has been a shift away from wars fought by "huge armies equipped with heavy conventional weapons" to wars waged "within, not between, states and by small armies mostly equipped with small arms and light weapons." These smaller-scale wars, although they can be extraordinarily brutal, usually generate far fewer casualties than conventional international wars.

Between 2001 and 2010, the number of major civil conflicts in Africa fell from seven to four. The continent has become so stable that in 2010 the consulting firm McKinsey & Company offered a bullish assessment for investments in Africa. The report was issued just before conflict erupted in Egypt and other northern African nations. But as of this writing, only the fighting in Libya appears to have killed more than one thousand people.

DOES DEMOCRACY PROMOTE PEACE?

Scholars have attributed the recent decline of war to various factors, some of which I have already critiqued. They include gender equality, prosperity, globalization (that is, capitalism plus international trade and investment), and the deterrent effects of nuclear weapons. One intriguing idea is that the surge in life expectancies, which have almost doubled over the last century in most regions, have made people more reluctant to risk their lives or the lives of their loved ones in armed conflicts.

As a journalist, I'd like to believe that the media has helped bring about the reduction of war. At its best, the media exposes the horror and hypocrisy of war. Photographs of children burned by napalm inflamed opposition to the Vietnam War, just as photographs of American guards taunting naked, terrified Iraqi prisoners in Abu Ghraib eroded support for the war in Iraq.

But of course leaders can all too easily employ the media to exploit our docility and bounded rationality, and our tendency to divide the world into "us" and "them." The Nazis used radio and newspapers to incite hatred of Jews and other groups. Broadcasts by Hutu leaders in Rwanda helped trigger the genocide against Tutsis in the early 1990s. The jingoism of American media after the 9/11 attacks helped George Bush make the case for invading Iraq. The media ia a problem as well as a solution.

The most popular explanation for the decline in war is the spread of democracy. I first heard about the link between democracy and peace in 1991, when the U.S. and its allies were trying to expel Iraq from Kuwait. Gloomy about the war, I sought out scholars trying to find solutions to militarism.

One is Bruce Russett, a professor of international relations and political science at Yale and editor (until 2009) of the *Journal of Conflict Resolution*. Russett was as disturbed by the Gulf War as I was; he felt that the U.S. should have given sanctions against Iraq more time to work before launching air strikes.

But he became excited telling me about the so-called democratic-peace phenomenon, which he called "perhaps the strongest non-trivial or non-tautological statement that can be made about international relations." Kant was the first scholar to propose a link between democracy and peace. The philosopher speculated that political leaders will become less likely to wage war as they become more accountable to their people, who always bear the brunt of war and hence will be more reluctant to fight.

Russett and other scholars started investigating Kant's thesis empirically in the 1980s, and they found evidence for democratic peace dating back to the early nineteenth century. Democracies, although they fight non-democracies, Russett says, "virtually never go to war with each other." The democratic-peace phenomenon implies that "anything we can do to further the spread of democracy will reduce the likelihood of war." It offers "the beginning of a vision of a world without war."

The spread of democracy correlates closely with the recent decline in international and civil wars. The nonprofit think tank Freedom House has charted the ebbs and flows of democracy around the world since the 1940s. Freedom House defines a nation as democratic, or "free," if it meets two criteria. First, it must "elect representatives who have a decisive impact on public policies and are accountable to the electorate." Second, the nation must allow "freedoms of expression and belief, associational and organizational rights, rule of law, and personal autonomy without interference from the state."

In its 2011 annual report, Freedom House categorizes eighty-seven of the world's 194 nations as "free" and another sixty as "partly free." People are "not free" in forty-seven countries, home to 34 percent of the global population. A single nation, China, accounts for roughly half of this percentage. The report states that global freedom declined in 2010 for the fifth consecutive year; twenty-five countries show decreased scores, and only eleven have increases. (The report does not address the Arab uprisings in early 2011.) But even with this backsliding, more people are living in genuine democracies than at any time in history. Only 12 percent of humanity lived under democratic rule in 1900 and 31 percent in 1950.

Now come the caveats. Democracies, needless to say, are not always paragons of peace, justice, and enlightenment. After French revolutionaries overthrew their corrupt monarchy at the end of the nineteenth century, they slaughtered thousands of their own people and, under Napoleon's leadership, embarked on wars of conquest against the rest of Europe. Throughout the nineteenth century European republics maltreated their colonial subjects. Americans slaughtered and stole the land of Native Americans; enslaved Africans; waged imperialist wars in the Philippines, Vietnam, Central America, and elsewhere; propped up dictatorial regimes that favored U.S. interests; and built up a nuclear arsenal that could destroy humanity, if not all life.

Moreover, democracies wage war in the name of democracy. U.S. officials cited democracy as a justification for invading Iraq in 2003, although this cause was invoked after the

original pretext—Iraq's alleged weapons of mass destruction—
had been exposed as fallacious. "The reason why I'm so strong
on democracy is democracies don't go to war with each other,"
George W. Bush stated in 2004. "And that's why I'm such a
strong believer that the way forward in the Middle East, the
broader Middle East, is to promote democracy."

Another problem—especially evident in Iraq and Afghanistan—is that "emerging" democracies, which still lack competent governments, legal institutions, and media, are often
wracked by violence and corruption. And finally, peoples'
yearning for freedom often culminates in deadly violence, as
demonstrated by the American and French Revolutions and
the recent revolts in Libya and other Arab nations. Democracy,
in other words—like capitalism, socialism, prosperity, and the
media—can be a problem as well as a solution.

JOHN MUELLER'S OPTIMISM

So why, then, have we been waging war less frequently since
World War II? My favorite explainer of this trend is John Mueller, a political scientist at Ohio State University. I met Mueller,
ironically, at the "Hybrid Warfare" conference I described in
the previous chapter. The organizer of that meeting, the historian and Army veteran Peter Mansoor, saw the recent decline in
war as just a temporary, random calm—like the one preceding
World War I—that will inevitably erupt once again into large-
scale violence.

Mueller rejects this fatalistic view. The most important
difference between our era and the early twentieth century, he

points out, is that we have learned from two world wars and countless other cataclysms that war is stupid, destructive, wasteful, and immoral. In short, wrong. As Mueller puts it in a 2009 paper, which echoes the thinking of Randall Forsberg, war is declining because "attitudes toward it have changed, roughly following the pattern according to which the ancient and once-formidable institution of formal, state-sponsored slavery became discredited and then obsolete."

Prior to World War I, Mueller points out, many prominent leaders and thinkers still extolled war as a progressive force in human evolution, which promoted the propagation of the fittest and winnowed out the weak. Kant wrote that "prolonged peace favors the predominance of a mere commercial spirit, and with it a debasing self-interest, cowardice and effeminacy." War "almost always enlarges the mind of a people and raises their character," the French historian Alexis de Tocqueville agreed. And Teddy Roosevelt declared at the end of the nineteenth century: "All the great masterful races have been fighting races. No triumph of peace is quite so great as the supreme triumph of war." Such glorifications of war became much less common after the horrific, industrial-scale carnage of World War I. Since then, Mueller notes, most leaders and pundits have tended to describe war as at best a necessary evil—a means to resist aggression and defend freedom—rather than an intrinsically good end in itself.

Like Margaret Mead, Mueller views war as a cultural "idea" or "invention" that has gripped humanity for millennia. War is "an institution," he writes, "that has been grafted onto human existence, rather than a trick of fate, a thunderbolt from hell, a natural calamity, a systemic necessity, or a desperate plot

contrivance dreamed up by some sadistic puppeteer up high."
He disagrees with Mead only on the point that we need to invent
something to replace war. We don't need to replace war with
anything, Mueller says. We just need to end it, and we seem to
be doing just that.

Mueller has been predicting the end of international war
since the late 1980s, when virtually no one took the idea seriously. He first contended that war between major powers was
becoming "obsolete" in his 1989 book *Retreat from Doomsday:
The Obsolescence of Major War*, published in timely fashion just
before the remarkably nonviolent collapse of the Soviet Union.
He has repeated and expanded upon this thesis since then in
a half dozen more books and scores of articles. "[W]e may be
reaching a point where war—in both its international and civil
varieties—ceases, or nearly ceases, to exist," he writes.

He acknowledges the fascination that war exerts over many
males. "There's this camaraderie," Mueller says, plus "the exhilaration of being in this dangerous area with adrenaline pumping
all the time." But he dismisses the idea that war is the inevitable
consequence of deep-rooted male compulsions. After war ends,
he points out, the vast majority of soldiers are relieved, not disappointed, when they go home and resume their civilian lives.
Neither the Swiss nor the Swedes have fought a battle in more
than two centuries, he adds, and "they don't seem hungry to get
back in it." The same is true of modern Japan and Germany.

Mueller is also skeptical of economic theories of war, noting that nations often fight not primarily for land, oil, or other
resources but for more emotional motives such as humiliation,
anger, and pride. The war between England and Argentina

over the tiny Falklands Islands in the 1980s was an example of a war fought almost solely for national honor. Many pundits have linked the recent decline of war to the spread of trade and democracy, but Mueller is dubious. Correlation does not equal causation, he says, and if anything, peace promotes trade and democracy rather than vice versa.

Nor is Mueller a great believer in arms control treaties, whether conventional or nuclear. Decreased international hostility, he suggests, is more likely to bring about disarmament rather than vice versa. Since the end of the cold war, France has gotten rid of two thirds of its nuclear weapons simply to save money. Mueller thinks that Britain may soon follow suit. Mueller discounts the view that nuclear weapons have deterred war between major powers. While nuclear weapons "may have been sufficient to prevent another major war, they have not been necessary to do so."

The memory of World Wars I and II and other major conflicts should provide sufficient deterrent for future international wars, he says. "Even allowing for stupidity, ineptness, miscalculation, and self-deception in these considerations, it does not appear that a large war, nuclear or otherwise, has been remotely in the interest of the essentially contented, risk-averse, escalation-anticipating powers that have dominated world affairs since 1945."

Mueller may not be as sanguine about the future as he sometimes sounds. If he were, why would he bother writing books and articles predicting the end of war? And he does admit to one major concern. Since 9/11, he says, the U.S. has "wildly over-reacted" to threats from terrorists. Over the past few decades, he notes, accidents involving home appliances and deer have killed more Americans than terrorists have. The 9/11 attacks provoked the U.S. into launching two wars, which so far have killed six thousand Americans—twice as many as died on 9/11—and tens of thousands of Iraqis and Afghans. The U.S. has also antagonized millions of Muslims around the world, exacerbating the problem it sought to solve. In other words, the biggest threat to peace is our excessive fear of war.

As Mueller would be the first to admit, peace is no more inevitable than war. We are still plagued by what Mueller describes as "the remnants of war," including terrorism, insurgencies, and criminal violence. He warns that attacks on civilians by "predatory militia bands in places like Sudan and Congo cause more damage and suffering than many wars." And the accidental or deliberate detonation of a single nuclear weapon could instantly reverse the recent decline in war-related casualties.

Also, I would add, leaders of the world's most powerful state still view war as legitimate under a wide range of circumstances. We keep spending more on preparations for war and finding new reasons to fight. In 2011, the Pentagon announced that it reserves the right to respond with bullets and bombs to "cyber war," digital attacks on U.S. communications and information systems. We revel in our victories over bullies like Hitler and Saddam Hussein. We cheer the news of the assassination of Osama bin Laden. We Americans glorify past wars, from the War of Independence to World War II. Far from reviling our veterans, for the most part we honor them, as I honor my father and grandfather.

I also think Mueller too quickly dismisses democracy as a

contributor to war's recent decline. Although democracy does not guarantee peace, I find the correlation in the decline of war and the surge of democracy over the past half-century striking. Peace could foster democracy rather than vice versa, as Mueller suggests, but the reverse could be true as well. As people gain more power over their own destiny, they seem to be choosing peace over war and prodding their leaders to do the same, as Kant predicted. After all, ordinary citizens rather than leaders always bear the brunt of war. Peace will certainly be more robust if it stems from the will of citizens and not just the whim of tyrants.

These concerns aside, I find Mueller's optimistic analysis persuasive, and inspiring. He convinces me that we can achieve a peaceful, largely disarmed world without first transforming it in other dramatic ways. To abolish war, he assures me, "you don't have to get rid of weapons. You don't have to change testosterone levels. You don't have to change social balances. Don't have to democratize. Don't have to become capitalist. Don't have to have trade. You don't have to have any of those things." We just have to want war to end, and to believe we can end it. The choice is ours. We are apparently already making this choice. Far from being a temporary, statistical anomaly, like a quiescent hurricane season, the decline of war reflects our growing aversion to war.

PEACE IS THE WAY

Throughout this book, I've examined attempts by scholars to identify factors especially conducive for peace. But there seem to be no conditions that, in and of themselves, inoculate a society against militarism. Not small government nor big government. Not democracy, socialism, capitalism, Christianity, Islam, Buddhism, nor secularism. Not giving equal rights to women or minorities nor reducing poverty. The contagion of war can infect any kind of society.

Some scholars, like the political scientist Joshua Goldstein, find this conclusion dispiriting. Early in his career Goldstein investigated economic theories of war, including those of Marx and Malthus. He concluded that war causes economic inequality and scarcity of resources as much as it stems from them. Goldstein, a self-described "pro-feminist," then set out to test whether macho, patriarchal attitudes caused armed violence. He felt so strongly about this thesis that he and his wife limited their son's exposure to violent media and contact sports.

But by the time he finished writing his 522-page book *War and Gender* in 2001, Goldstein had rejected the thesis. He questioned many of his initial assumptions about the causes of war. He never gave credence to explanations involving innate male aggression—war breaks out too sporadically for that—but he saw no clear-cut evidence for non-biological factors either. "War is not a product of capitalism, imperialism, gender, innate aggression, or any other single cause, although all of these influence wars' outbreaks and outcomes," Goldstein writes. "Rather, war has in part fueled and sustained these and other injustices." He admits that all his research has left him "somewhat more pessimistic about how quickly or easily war may end."

But here is the upside of this insight: if there are no conditions that in and of themselves prevent war, there are none that make peace impossible, either. This is the source of John

Mueller's optimism, and mine. If we want peace badly enough, we can have it, no matter what kind of society we live in. The choice is ours. And once we have escaped from the shadow of war, we will have more resources to devote to other problems that plague us, like economic injustice, poor health, and environmental destruction, which war often exacerbates.

The Waorani, whose abandonment of war led to increased trade and intermarriage, are a case in point. So is Costa Rica. In 2010, this Central American country was ranked number one out of 148 nations in a "World Database of Happiness" compiled by Dutch sociologists, who gathered information on the self-reported happiness of people around the world. Costa Rica also received the highest score in another "happiness" survey, carried out by an American think tank, that factored in the nation's impact on the environment. The United States was ranked twentieth and 114th, respectively, on the surveys. Instead of spending on arms, over the past half century Costa Rica's government invested in education, as well as healthcare, environmental conservation, and tourism, all of which helped make the country more prosperous, healthy, and happy. There is no single way to peace, but peace is the way to solve many other problems.

The research of Mueller, Goldstein, Forsberg, and other scholars yields one essential lesson. Those of us who want to make the world a better place—more democratic, equitable, healthier, cleaner—should make abolishing the invention of war our priority, because peace can help bring about many of the other changes we seek. This formula turns on its head the old social activists' slogan: "If you want peace, work for justice." I say instead, "If you want justice, work for peace." If you want less pollution, more money for healthcare and education, an improved legal and political system—work for peace.

CHAPTER SIX

The Power of Nonviolence

In the summer of 2005, I received an email that read: "The U.S. National Counterterrorism Center is seeking your help in the global war on terror. We are looking for novel ideas that will advance the analysis of counterterrorism." I assumed it was a joke, or a case of mistaken identity. When I called a contact listed in the message, a woman who identified herself as "Debbie" informed me that the message was legitimate. Her employer, a defense contractor called Centra, was helping the Counterrorism Center, a security agency overseen by the CIA, solicit ideas from "non-experts" who can "think outside the box."

I was ambivalent, to put it mildly. If my country was asking me for advice, its War on Terror was in even worse shape than I imagined. I also worried that, as someone who reviles the Bush administration's hawkish policies, I'd be a hypocrite to accept this assignment. But the assignment paid reasonably well, and I doubted whether I'd get another opportunity to give the administration a piece of my mind, so I wrote up a few ideas. They included interviewing retired members of the Irish Republican Army for insights into how terrorists plan attacks, using artificial-intelligence programs to find patterns in past terrorist attacks and thereby predict future ones, and disseminating the writings of Gene Sharp to groups at risk of resorting to violence.

Centra accepted all of my proposals except for the last one, which Debbie called "too political" to pass on to the Counterterrorism Center. But that's the proposal I thought would be most effective. To my mind, our best hope for making the transition from an unjust, militarized world to a just, peaceful one is for people seeking social change to do so nonviolently. Sharp's entire career has been devoted to showing would-be activists just how powerful nonviolence can be and advising them on how to employ it.

The potential of Sharp's ideas became much better known in the first few months of 2011, after largely nonviolent protests toppled the repressive, corrupt governments of Tunisia and Egypt. The latter, headed for decades by strongman Hosni Mubarak, had been one of the world's most brutal regimes. Organizers of the successful uprisings, the *New York Times* reported, were influenced by Sharp's writings. The *Times* described Sharp as a "shy," "stoop-shouldered," eighty-three-year-old running a chronically underfunded think tank in Boston called the Albert Einstein Institution. "For the world's despots," the *Times* added, "his ideas can be fatal."

A 2008 profile in the *Wall Street Journal* credits Sharp with "helping to advance a global democratic awakening."

His writings have influenced opposition movements in Serbia, Ukraine, Georgia, Kyrgyzstan, Russia, Burma, Palestine, Venezuela, and Iran as well as Tunisia and Egypt. Sharp has been denounced by officials in some of these countries. Iranian officials view him as such a serious threat that they produced a bizarre animated video of "senior White House official" John McCain, "Jewish tycoon" George Soros, and "CIA agent" Sharp in the White House plotting the overthrow of Iran.

He published his first major work, *The Politics of Nonviolent Action*, in 1973 while teaching political science at Harvard. Since then, he has steadily churned out more books, papers, and pamphlets describing how people can bring about political change nonviolently. His writings, which have been translated into more than thirty languages and are available on the internet, describe a wide variety of tactics: worker strikes, student strikes, mass petitions, underground newspapers, skywriting, display of flags and banners, boycotts of goods, boycotts of sporting events, refusal to pay rent, withdrawal of bank savings, fasts, mock trials, occupation of government buildings, marches, motorcades, teach-ins, pray-ins, ostracism of collaborators, publication of names of collaborators, seeking imprisonment, formation of parallel government, and mass disrobing. Many of Sharp's methods involve mockery, which the !Kung and other hunter-gatherer groups also employ against the swell-headed.

A major goal of Sharp's work is to get people to realize that they have more power—more choices—than they think they do. Even the most brutal tyrants must rely to some extent on the cooperation of citizens, not just those serving as soldiers and police but throughout the society. Sharp is not the first person to offer this insight. After asking how thirty thousand Englishmen "subdued" 200 million Indians, the pacifist Russian novelist Leo Tolstoy responded: "Do not the figures make it clear that it is not the English who have enslaved the Indians, but the Indians who have enslaved themselves?" Gandhi, similarly, wrote that ending British rule required convincing Indians to "consider it a shame to assist or cooperate with a government that had forfeited all title to respect or support."

Sharp is not a gentle or diplomatic man. When I interviewed him in Boston in 2003, he spoke in a low, gravelly growl, which made him seem even more blunt and curmudgeonly. Sharp was a Quaker and conscientious objector in the 1950s, and was imprisoned for refusing to serve in the Korean War. His greatest influences are Gandhi and Martin Luther King, whom he views as geniuses of nonviolent activism. But he now dismisses his conscientious objection as an ineffective gesture, and he accuses some pacifists of being more interested in demonstrating their moral purity than bringing about change. "If people want to be pacifists and conscientious objectors that's fine," he told me, "but don't think you're going to save the world that way."

Sharp advocates nonviolence for practical rather than spiritual reasons. He rejects religious exhortations that we should turn the other cheek and love our enemies. People in power often deserve to be despised and fought, he contends, but violence, even in the service of a just cause, often causes more problems than it solves, leading to greater injustice and suffering. Hence the best way to oppose an unjust regime, he says, is through nonviolent action. Nonviolent movements are also more likely than violent ones to garner internal and international support and to lead to democratic, non-militarized regimes.

Because of his emphasis on pragmatism—and his rough-edged manner—Sharp has antagonized some pacifists, who compare him to cold-hearted political theorists like Machiavelli and Clausewitz. Sharp makes no apologies for the fact that his strategies can be employed toward insidious as well as noble ends. A world in which bad people pursued their goals nonviolently, he points out, would be a vast improvement over ours.

Like John Mueller, Sharp discounts the value of international treaties. Nor is he keen on the idea of an armed, global government that enforces treaties and quashes violent movements. "We've seen what military capacities, and police intervention capacities, can become within a country," he said. "They are key tools of dictatorships, both for maintaining existing dictatorships and for establishing new ones. Now we want to extend that capacity on a world scale? And who is going to control the people who are giving the orders and making the decisions?" Sharp envisions, instead, world peace emerging from "an incremental increase in the use of non-violent struggle in the place of violence" in troubled regions around the world.

What I like most about Sharp's philosophy of nonviolence is that it is based on a clear-eyed view of human nature. When asked if he views humanity as fundamentally good-natured, Sharp laughs and shakes his head, muttering, "No, no, no." But he does believe that most people—even members of terrorist groups like al Qaeda—wage war not for its own sake but as a means to an end; if they can be persuaded that nonviolence is more effective than violence, they will choose nonviolence.

THE UNITED NATIONS AND OTHER SOLUTIONS

Realists often accuse proponents of nonviolence of naïveté and wishful thinking, and they tend to agree with Mao Zedong that "political power grows out of the barrel of a gun." But history offers abundant evidence of the power of nonviolent methods, even against ruthless regimes. In 494 BCE, working-class plebeians in Rome, protesting their treatment at the hands of the Roman consuls, staged a kind of sit-down strike on a hill near the city, later called the Sacred Mount. They remained there for several days, disrupting life in Rome, until the consuls acceded to many of their demands. Roman soldiers employed a similar nonviolent strategy more than two hundred years later to win concessions from the Roman Senate.

In Nazi-occupied Norway in 1942, Norway's puppet leader, Vidkun Quisling, ordered Norwegian teachers to join a "corporation" that would promote fascist principles. As many as ten thousand of Norway's twelve thousand teachers refused to join the organization and signed statements of protest against it. Quisling had one thousand teachers arrested and sent to concentration camps, but the others maintained their resistance. Quisling finally gave in, allowing the imprisoned teachers to return home.

In their 2000 book *A Force More Powerful: A Century of Nonviolent Conflict*, Peter Ackerman, a political scientist, and Jack

DuVall, a journalist, document many other cases of nonviolent activism in the twentieth century. Some of their examples, especially those involving charismatic leaders, are well known. Gandhi's organization of boycotts, strikes, and other acts of civil disobedience against the British Empire. Martin Luther King's marches against segregation and other legally sanctioned forms of racism. The triumph of Nelson Mandela and the African National Congress over white rule in South Africa. (The ANC had a military branch early on but gradually embraced nonviolence.) The rebellion of Wałesa and Polish labor unionists against the totalitarian control of the Soviet Union.

Largely nonviolent movements also helped topple dictatorships in East Germany, Mongolia, the Philippines, Chile, Argentina, and elsewhere. These cases, Ackerman and DuVall point out, show that nonviolent methods "can end oppression and liberate nations and people, and they can do so with less risk and more certainty than resorting to violent revolt or terror." Pessimists often forget these instances in which ostensibly powerless people prevailed over violent regimes without the use of force.

Take away these success stories, and the twentieth century would have been far bloodier. We should also give more conventional conflict-resolution methods, such as international diplomacy, their due. Take, for example, the Camp David Accords, which Egypt and Israel signed in 1978, just five years after the two nations had battled each other in the Yom Kippur War. The Egyptian President Anwar el-Sadat and the Israeli Prime Minister Menachem Begin agreed on the treaty after secret negotiations overseen by President Jimmy Carter. Begin and el-Sadat shared the 1978 Nobel Peace Prize for their agreement.

Many scholars also give the United Nations credit for suppressing global violence since its founding in 1945. Like its precursor, the League of Nations, the U.N. has failed to prevent many wars. U.N. officials have been accused of financial corruption and peacekeeping troops of rape, robbery, and other crimes against those they are supposed to protect. The Nobel Foundation nonetheless gave its Peace Prize to the U.N. Peacekeeping Forces in 1988, stating they have "played a significant role in reducing the level of conflict even though the fundamental causes of the struggles frequently remain." A 2007 analysis by RAND Corporation concluded that the U.N. has provided much more cost-efficient peacekeeping and nation-building than the United States.

"It would be depressing to catalogue the many failures of the United Nations," the political journalist Gwynne Dyer writes, "but it would also be misleading." Dyer gives the U.N. partial credit for the absence of wars between major powers since World War II. He adds that "wars that have broken out between middle-sized powers from time to time—Arab–Israeli wars and Indo–Pakistani wars, mostly—seldom lasted more than a month, because the U.N.'s offers of ceasefires and peacekeeping troops offered a way out for the losing side." In short, we don't need to invent brand new institutions for keeping the peace. We just need to improve the ones we have.

NICARAGUA VERSUS COSTA RICA

In 1985, I witnessed firsthand the difference between a militarized and demilitarized culture when I spent a month in Nicaragua. At that time, the tiny Central American nation was controlled by the sandinistas, socialist revolutionaries who in 1979 had toppled a U.S. backed dictator, Anastasio Somoza. I traveled to Nicaragua to learn more about the sandinistas and their battle against U.S. sponsored insurgents, called contras.

Nicaragua was swarming with soldiers and police, who—not surprisingly, given my American appearance—often stopped me to ask for my passport and inquire about the reason for my visit. At night in Estelí, the northern town where I spent most of my trip, I could occasionally hear the crack and boom of small-arms fire and mortars from skirmishes between sandinistas and contras near the border with Honduras. Other signs of war were ubiquitous, including funeral processions and people missing limbs—blown off, the Nicaraguan family I was staying with told me, by Contra mines or mortar shells.

Before landing in Nicaragua, I spent two days in Costa Rica. The contrast between the two countries, which geographically and ethnically are almost identical, was striking. Costa Rica felt like a tranquil, lovely paradise, and compared to Nicaragua it was. Costa Ricans had worked hard to keep their country from being infected by the wars raging elsewhere in Central America since they abolished their army in 1949.

When Óscar Arias was elected President of Costa Rica in 1986, one of his first acts—carried out in defiance of President Ronald Reagan—was to prohibit contras from using Costa Rica as a base for attacks against Nicaragua. That same year, Arias promoted a plan to reduce violence and promote democracy in Nicaragua, El Salvador, Honduras, and Guatemala, which were then wracked by civil wars. The plan, which was eventually accepted by all of Costa Rica's neighbors, is credited with helping quell (although certainly not extinguish) armed conflict in these nations.

In 1987, Arias won the Nobel Peace Prize for this work. In his acceptance speech, he acknowledged that Costa Rica's commitment to demilitarization was constantly tested. The persistence of extreme poverty, political instability, and violence in Central America, he pointed out, led some Costa Ricans to advocate bringing back armed forces as protection. "Apocalyptic prophets abound," Arias said, "announcing the failures of the fight against poverty, proclaiming the immediate fall of the democracies, forecasting the futility of peace-making efforts. I do not share this defeatism. I cannot accept to be realistic means to tolerate misery, violence, and hate." The key to achieving peace in a still violent world, Arias understood, is resisting fear and fatalism.

DAMNED-IF-YOU-DO-OR-DON'T DILEMMAS

Of course, sometimes attempts to resolve conflicts nonviolently fail. The recent Arab uprisings are a case in point. After protesters in Tunisia and Egypt ousted their repressive governments in early 2011 without large-scale bloodshed, the limits of nonviolent resistance became apparent, as government forces crushed protest movements in Libya, Syria, Bahrain, and Yemen. The crackdown of Libya's leader, Qaddafi, on his citizens was especially brutal. The U.S. and other nations faced the familiar, agonizing dilemma: should they employ force to protect Libyans from Qaddafi, and risk making the situation worse, or just allow Qaddafi to continue killing his own people?

History abounds in these damned-if-you-do-or-don't dilemmas. Should American colonialists have violently resisted British rule? Should Lincoln have waged war to preserve the Union and end slavery? Should the U.S. and other nations have intervened when Saddam Hussein seized Kuwait in 1990? When Serbians carried out ethnic cleansing against Albanians in Kosovo? When Hutus started slaughtering Tutsis in Rwanda? When China squashed Tibet's attempts to gain independence? Let's say that Nazi Germany had not invaded any other countries but had carried out its plan to exterminate all German Jews. Should other nations have attempted to stop the slaughter? When, if ever, is nonviolence less moral than violence?

These are the quandaries that Just War theory purports to answer. Just War theory has a checkered history. One of its founders, the fourth-century cleric Saint Augustine, was keen on holy wars waged by Christians against infidels. He argued that killing sinners and non-believers is righteous, because it stops them from sinning. This logic helped inspire the Crusades and European conquests in the Americas. Just War theorists have also reasoned that war, because it is so awful, should be waged ruthlessly to end it as quickly as possible. This logic justified Sherman's brutal devastation of the South during the Civil War, Churchill's decision to bomb civilian populations in Germany, and Truman's choice to drop atomic bombs on Japan.

Virtually all modern warriors claim—and even believe— that their cause is just. Some wars, especially "humanitarian interventions" undertaken to help others, are less wrong than others. But in the bad barrel of war, even warriors fighting for the noblest of causes almost invariably commit horrific crimes. The armed intervention of the U.S. and its NATO allies against Qaddafi demonstrates this truth. Bombs dropped by NATO planes have killed not only Qaddafi's troops, but also the civilians and armed rebels NATO is supposed to be protecting. The Libyan rebels, after gaining the upper hand in certain towns, reportedly killed civilians loyal to Qaddafi, prompting reprisals from Qaddafi loyalists. NATO's attacks, like all acts of war, also legitimize militarism as a means of solving problems.

THE LIMITS OF (MY) PACIFISM

Pacifists consider the concept of a "just" war to be an oxymoron. Needless to say, I'm sympathetic toward this viewpoint. I've come to believe that all wars are choices. None are truly necessary. NATO's intervention in Libya certainly wasn't. Bombing Libya, I believe, was a mistake. But I relate to the Obama administration's empathy for and desire to help helpless civilians being attacked by a cruel bully. Could I have stood by if I had the power to stop, or try to stop, Qaddafi?

I realize, upon reading about acts of true pacifism, that my commitment to nonviolence has limits. In a 2003 essay, the Quaker Alastair McIntosh recalls living in a "beautiful but violent third-world country" when young men from a squatter camp abducted and gang-raped the seventeen-year-old daughter of a Quaker friend. Rather than report the men to the police, McIntosh, his friend, and the daughter told leaders of the camp what had happened. The leaders arranged for members of the community, including the rapists, to turn out en masse to apologize to the girl and her father.

Noting that some of the rapists "had tears in their eyes" during the ceremony, McIntosh writes, "You just knew that, whilst the re-offending rate might not be zero, it would be very much less" than had they been violently punished. I believe in the healing power of love and forgiveness, and I appreciate McIntosh's point that even when confronted with savage brutality, we don't have to respond in kind. We have more choices than we think we do. But I would never choose as these Quakers did. Reason and emotion alike tell me that violent criminals—even if they aren't irredeemable psychopaths—should be imprisoned to prevent them from repeating their crime and to deter others.

Nor can I accept McIntosh's argument that a genuine commitment to nonviolence entails "preferring to die than to kill." That's why I've always been disturbed by Gandhi's proposal for resisting hostile armed forces—such as Japanese armies that threatened India during World War II—with "peace armies" consisting primarily of women and children. At first, Gandhi asserts, the soldiers may bayonet or shoot these passive resistors, but eventually the aggressors will relent and hurl down their arms in self-loathing. And if they don't, at least those who die will not have stooped to the level of the killers. "The non-violent resistors will have won the day," Gandhi writes, "inasmuch as they will have preferred extermination to submission." Gandhi seems to suggest that individual lives are worth sacrificing for the larger principle of nonviolence. This attitude strikes me as all too similar to that of leaders who urge us to lay down our lives for God and country.

Pacifists like McIntosh and Gandhi have faith that empathy can be aroused even in hardened, hateful killers if they are confronted with love rather than violence. But history shows that individuals, groups, and entire nations can become psychopathic, slaughtering innocents without remorse. Prior to the rise of the Nazis, Einstein was an outspoken pacifist. He rejected Just War theory, arguing that one "does not make wars less likely to occur by formulating rules to warfare." Speaking in the U.S. in 1930, he urged audiences to refuse to participate in military service. After the Nazi invasion of Belgium, however, Einstein announced that if he were Belgian he would "cheerfully" sign up for military service. The Nazis had to be opposed by force "to save European civilization."

One veteran anti-war activist who agonized over damned-if-you-do-or-don't dilemmas was the historian Howard Zinn, whose attitude toward war was shaped by his service as a bombardier during World War II. Just weeks before Germany surrendered in 1945, Zinn flew in a bombing raid on German-occupied towns in France. Later, he learned that the raids had incinerated French civilians as well as German soldiers. Zinn suspects that U.S. commanders ordered the raid, which given Germany's imminent defeat was probably unnecessary, to test out a new explosive: jellied gasoline, otherwise known as napalm. Yes, the Nazis had to be opposed, Zinn told me when I interviewed him in 2003. But no cause, he said, no matter how righteous, justifies killing civilians.

"I don't call myself a pacifist," Zinn told me. "I don't believe in absolutes." There are times, he acknowledges, when a "small degree of force" might be required to prevent greater violence. He felt, for example, that the U.N. should have intervened to prevent genocide in Rwanda in the early 1990s. But he opposed almost all other armed interventions, like those in Korea, Vietnam, Iraq in 1991 and 2003, and Afghanistan. Zinn insisted that we must, and can, find better ways to solve damned-if-you-do-or-don't dilemmas. In his autobiography he writes: "I see this as the central issue of our time: how to find a substitute for war in human ingenuity, imagination, courage, sacrifice, patience."

JUST POLICING

I believe people have the right to defend themselves against violent attacks. We also have the right, and sometimes the duty, to help others being threatened by bullies. But given war's terrible unpredictability, and its tendency to exacerbate rather than solve problems, we should do all we can to alleviate damned-if-you-do-or-don't dilemmas nonviolently—or, if that fails, with minimal force. I don't have any special formula for determining exactly when and how to use force. I just have a few simple—simplistic, some might say—rules.

First, we should heed the Hippocratic command to do no harm. In other words, whatever we do, we shouldn't make a bad situation worse, which is just what the U.S. and its allies have done in Afghanistan, Iraq, and Libya. We should stop using mines, bombs, and other weapons that kill indiscriminately. That includes the drones that the Obama administration has deployed to carry out assassinations in Iraq, Afghanistan, Pakistan, Yemen, and probably elsewhere.

Minimizing casualties, even among combatants, should be the highest priority. The manner in which police employ force should be the model. In the U.S. and most other democratic countries, police are legally required to avoid hurting civilians and even criminals. If police know that a psychotic, armed killer is holding hostages in a building, they don't immediately bomb the building or storm it with machine guns blazing. In fact, they try to capture rather than kill the killer, so that he can be tried by the justice system. Often, this means that police patiently try to talk the criminal into surrendering without hurting his hostages. Zinn perhaps had such strategies in mind when he included "patience" as a substitute for war.

The principle of minimizing civilian casualties should also apply to ostensibly nonviolent interventions, such as economic sanctions. U.S. sanctions against Iraq in the 1990s—which included bans on imports of medical and agricultural supplies—reportedly led to the deaths of hundreds of thousands of Iraqi children. In an episode of *60 Minutes* aired on May 12, 1996, correspondent Lesley Stahl asked Madeleine Albright, then the American ambassador to the U.N., about the sanctions against Iraq.

"We have heard that a half million children have died," Stahl said. "I mean, that's more children than died in Hiroshima. And, you know, is the price worth it?" Albright replied: "I think this is a very hard choice, but the price—we think the price is worth it." Later, after becoming Secretary of State, Albright called her response to Stahl's question "a terrible mistake, hasty, clumsy, and wrong. Nothing matters more than the lives of innocent people." Albright was right the second time.

The approach I'm recommending resembles the "just policing" advocated by the theologian Gerald Schlabach. He sees three key differences between police work and conventional warfare. I've already mentioned two: police officers place the safety of civilians above all other goals, and they strive not to kill criminals but to bring them to justice. The third difference identified by Schlabach is rhetorical. Whereas wartime leaders often employ charged, emotional language to rally a nation against the enemy, competent police officials seek to tamp down rather than inflame emotions.

THE END-OF-WAR RULE

These rules are restrictive enough, but I have one more that, if followed, may result in even fewer armed interventions: whatever our response is to a damned-if-you-do-or-don't dilemma, we should formulate it with the larger goal of abolishing war, and even the threat of war, once and for all. This means that, if we employ violence, we must do so in a way that does not legitimize violence as a solution to problems. This may seem to be a tricky, even impossible, proposition, but police pull it off when they're doing their jobs well.

The end-of-war rule demands that we consider not only the immediate consequences of our actions but also how they will be perceived by others. Will our actions be viewed as disproportionately violent? Will they provoke reprisals? Will our intervention, which we claim is purely altruistic, look to others like muscle-flexing? A demonstration of our nifty new stealth fighter or drone? A reminder to other nations around the world of our overwhelming military superiority? An attempt to seize oil reserves? Are our actions consistent with the principle that war is immoral and needs to be abolished? Or will our actions make it easier for other groups to justify their violence?

These questions are directed primarily at the U.S., which—let's face it—is the world's biggest problem and solution. I love my country, but I am often embarrassed by the chasm between our lofty rhetoric and our actions. We denounce al Qaeda, rightly, for the moral nihilism and illegitimacy that it demonstrates when it kills thousands of innocent American civilians. So how does the U.S. respond to 9/11? By invading two countries and killing thousands of civilians who had nothing to do with the attacks.

We claim to revere peace and human rights—and yet we keep embarking on unnecessary wars, in which we treat alleged enemies and even civilians cruelly. We pay lip service to the principles of national sovereignty and international law while secretly carrying out deadly commando raids and drone attacks around the world. We sell weapons to other nations, and to their adversaries. We prop up dictators if they let us build military bases on their land, exploit their cheap labor, or sell us their oil and other resources at low prices. We are guilty of shameful hypocrisy. If we practiced what we preached—if we showed through our actions that we recognize how wrong war is—we Americans could lead the entire world to an enduring peace.

We could start by slashing our bloated military, abolishing arms sales to other countries, and getting rid of our nuclear arsenal. These steps, rather than empty rhetoric, will encourage other countries to demilitarize as well. To show our commitment to the principle of nonviolence, we should ban capital punishment, as most nations have already done. Like war, capital punishment is a gross contradiction. To show that killing is wrong, we kill killers. I oppose capital punishment not because I feel empathy for murderers but because this sanctioned form of violence demeans us and makes us hypocrites, just as war does.

With imaginative, courageous leadership, we may soon live in a largely disarmed world, in which war between any two nations becomes inconceivable. Most nations will need only lightly armed police forces to protect citizens against the violent cults, criminal gangs, and psychopaths that might occasionally spring up in their midst. The international community might also want to maintain a small force that can help counter international threats. The best organization for carrying out international police interventions is the United Nations.

Perhaps it's too much to expect warriors to envision a warless world, but some pull off this feat. Paul Chappell is a U.S. Army captain who graduated from West Point in 2002 and served in Iraq in 2006 and 2007. In two essays published in 2009 and 2010, he describes how he grew up in the shadow of war. His father, who served in Korea and Vietnam, suffered from post-traumatic stress disorder, which provoked violent rages and depression.

When Chappell was in eighth grade, he asked a teacher, "Where does war come from?" She answered that war happens because people are "naturally evil." Her answer made no sense to Chappell. If people are so prone to violence, he thought, why does war traumatize so many soldiers, like his father? His readings on warfare, and his personal experiences as a soldier, eventually convinced Chappell that warriors are motivated primarily not by innate aggression but by affection for their comrades and fellow citizens.

Chappell predicts that, as humans learn to extend their innate empathy and altruism to all others, war will fade away, sometime in this century. The profession of soldiering will not vanish entirely but will evolve. As a possible model, Chappell upholds the New Zealand armed forces, which train primarily to provide relief to victims of natural disasters, including earthquakes, tsunamis, famines, and epidemics. Soldiers in a post-war world should be called "protectors," Chappell proposes, because they are willing to risk their lives to help protect others. When my teenage son Mac told me recently that he was considering becoming a soldier, I was dismayed, but I would be proud if he served as a protector in a post-war world.

HARNESSING THE POWER OF RELIGION

I'd like to return for a moment to the question of pacifism, and especially religiously inspired pacifism. A group of intellectuals collectively known as the "new atheists" argue that the world would be better off without religion. That is the theme of *The God Delusion* by Richard Dawkins, *The End of Faith* by the neuroscientist Sam Harris, and *God Is Not Good* by the journalist Christopher Hitchens. At times, I'm inclined to agree that the harm done by religious folk outweighs the good works they also do. All the world's great religions, in principle, encourage us to behave altruistically toward others, but in practice they often result in lethal intolerance. Faith motivates al Qaeda and other terrorist groups and exacerbates conflicts in Iraq, Afghanistan, the Middle East, and elsewhere.

Religion can also lead to fatalistic attitudes toward war, even in sophisticated believers. A case in point is the geneticist and born-again Christian Francis Collins. Former director of the Human Genome Project and current director of the National Institutes of Health, he is one of the most influential scientists in the world. I once asked Collins if he thinks science has the potential to solve the problem of war, as well as cancer and other diseases. Collins shook his head. No matter how much science progresses, he said, we will remain sinners, who "kill each other out of our self-righteousness and our determination that we have to be on top." Collins has more faith in science and God than in humankind.

On the other hand, the number of people killed in religious conflicts over the past century is dwarfed by those exterminated in the name of secular ideologies like communism, capitalism, and fascism. Moreover, religion is not going to vanish any time soon, particularly in the U.S., the most powerful nation on Earth. Bashing religious people for their foolishness and hypocrisy, as the new atheists do, may even be counterproductive. This aggressive stance may make the faithful defensive and hostile toward secular, scientific values, and it may alienate agnostics and others who fall into a middle ground between faith and anti-religious atheism.

Edward O. Wilson, who was raised as a Southern Baptist before becoming a world-famous biologist at Harvard, takes a more constructive approach to religion than the new atheists. Over the past few decades, his great mission has been preserving the astoundingly diverse species on our planet. In his 2006 book *The Creation*, written in the form of a letter to an evangelical minister, Wilson asks Christians to join him in working to preserve God's creation, life on Earth.

In the same way, secular anti-war activists can reach out to religious people and seek to enlist them in the cause of abolishing war, especially those who often support hawkish, aggressive policies in spite of their scriptures' prohibitions against cruelty and violence. Think how quickly war would end if believers and non-believers united to abolish it!

REJECTING DEFEATISM

Because words and ideas matter, our leaders—whether religious, scientific, or political—should also reject, once and for all, the stance that wars are inevitable. Politicians like Barack Obama have a special duty to help us overcome our feelings of despair and envision a peaceful future—even if their own faith is weak. The model I have in mind is a commencement speech that President John F. Kennedy gave at American University in 1963, shortly before his assassination. Kennedy urged his young audience to reject the "dangerous, defeatist belief" that "war is inevitable, that mankind is doomed, that we are gripped by forces we cannot control. We need not accept that view. Our problems are manmade—therefore, they can be solved by man."

Defeatism can seep into the thinking of even our most eloquent anti-war writers, like the novelist and journalist William

Vollmann. His magnum opus is a massive, seven-volume meditation on violence, *Rising Up and Rising Down* (published by the same house that produced the book you hold in your hands). Vollmann presents every conceivable damned-if-you-do-or-don't dilemma, and he struggles mightily to derive a "moral calculus" for computing when violence is justified on a personal, national, or international level. Individuals and nations have the right to defend themselves against violent attacks, Vollmann allows, but should they resort to force to defend others? To prevent mass rape? Infanticide? Slavery? Torture? Starvation? When, if ever, is killing civilians justified? What about enemy soldiers who have surrendered?

Vollmann's book is one long cry of despair. He agonizes over each dilemma, resisting easy answers—because of course there are none. The only solution, I believe, is to create a world in which we rarely, if ever, wage war to stop war or other atrocities. Vollmann rules out this possibility, declaring that "to murder is not only human, but protohuman" and that "human violence itself cannot be altered without altering human nature." War will only end, he says, "if thermonuclear war exterminates all of us." He confesses that "putting aside any notion that the world is becoming a better place was neither easy nor pleasant for me."

I must respectfully disagree, Mr. Vollmann. We are not innately murderous, and the world is clearly becoming a better place. When my grandparents were young, American women did not have the right to vote, segregation was still legal, and lynching was still common in the South. I grew up in the shadow of the Vietnam War, but I did not have to fight in a cataclysmic World War, as my grandfather and father did. My children and students did not grow up fearing, as I did as a boy, that at any moment a global nuclear war could destroy all of humanity and even all life on Earth.

Over the past century, most nations have shifted away from monarchy and other forms of authoritarian rule and toward democracy. Life expectancies have soared, and the proportion of people afflicted by extreme, life-threatening poverty has plummeted. Humanity is healthier, more prosperous, and freer than it has ever been. Advances in science, technology, medicine, politics, and all other spheres of life are objective, empirical facts. We are facing fewer damned-if-you-do-or-don't dilemmas, because we are learning to resolve our disputes nonviolently. "No one knows enough to be a pessimist," Norman Cousins wrote once. I'd go further: we know enough to be optimists, especially about the prospects for global peace.

In Defense of Free Will

War is not the only obsession I inflict on my students. Free will is another. No matter what class I'm teaching—"War and Human Nature," "History of Science and Technology," "Seminar in Science Writing"—sooner or later I end up talking about free will. The two issues are closely related. You are less likely to see war as a choice—as something that we make happen rather than something that happens to us—if you doubt whether choices of any kind are really possible.

To my dismay, many leading scientists view free will as an illusion. "It is hard to imagine how free will can operate if our behavior is determined by physical law," the physicists Stephen Hawking and Leonard Mlodinow declare in a recent book, "so it seems that we are no more than biological machines and that free will is just an illusion." Even Einstein, the most humane of scientists, doubted free will. He once wrote that if "the moon were gifted with self-consciousness, it would feel thoroughly convinced that it was traveling its way of its own accord."

Einstein and Hawking are physicists, who may be more prone to determinism. I'm more disturbed by the skepticism toward free will expressed by Francis Crick, the co-discoverer of the double helix. Crick, who spent the last decades of his life studying the brain, once tried to talk me out of my belief in free will. Picking up a pen from his desk, he noted that even this simple act was underpinned and preceded by complex bio-chemical processes that take place below the level of conscious-ness. "What you're aware of is a decision," he explained, "but you're not aware of what makes you do the decision. It seems free to you, but it's the result of things you're not aware of."

Crick was one of the smartest people I've ever met, but he was wrong about free will. Like many other free will deniers, he cited experiments carried out in the 1980s by the psycholo-gist Benjamin Libet. Libet asked subjects to push a button at a moment of their choosing while noting the time of their decision as displayed on a clock. Subjects took one fifth of a second, on average, to push the button after they decided to do so. But an electroencephalograph (EEG) monitoring the sub-jects' brain waves revealed a spike of activity almost a second before the subjects decided to push the button. This and other findings show that our conscious decisions are literally after-thoughts, according to Crick and other neuroscientists. "Our belief in free will," Sam Harris contends in his 2010 best seller *The Moral Landscape*, "arises from our moment-to-moment ignorance of specific prior causes."

EEGs are a crude measure of neural activity, but in 2011 neuroscientists led by Itzhak Fried replicated Libet's results with electrodes implanted directly into the brain. Fried's group inserts electrodes into epileptics' brains to pinpoint the epicenters of their seizures, which are then surgically removed. While gathering this clinical information, Fried's team, after getting patients' permission, had them perform the Libet experiment. The electrodes revealed a burst of activity in the supplementary motor area of patients' brains—which underpins the decision to act—as much as one and a half seconds before the patients actually pressed the button.

"So it turns out that there are neurons in your brain that know you are about to make a movement the better part of a second before you know it yourself," the cognitive scientists Daniela Schiller and David Carmel comment in *Scientific American*. "It might be tempting to conclude that free will is an illusion." I choose to resist this temptation. Libet's clock experiment is a lousy probe of free will, because the subject has made the decision in advance to push the button; the only question is the timing. I would be more surprised if the EEG sensors or implanted electrodes did *not* detect any neural build-up to the subject's action.

I'm more impressed by implant experiments that reveal how we fool ourselves into thinking we're in control when we're not. Scientists can make a patient's arm shoot into the air, for example, by electrically stimulating a spot in the motor cortex. The patient often insists that she meant to move the arm and even invents a reason why: she was waving to that handsome doctor! In his 2002 book *The Illusion of Conscious Will*, the psychologist Daniel Wegner calls these delusional, after-the-fact explanations "confabulations."

We all confabulate now and then. We docilely do what we're told to do—and believe what we're told to believe—by parents, priests, and presidents, and we convince ourselves it's our choice. We subvert our wills by deliberating insincerely, toward a foregone conclusion, and by failing to act upon our resolutions. Sometimes we act out of compulsion—out of fear or rage—without thinking through the consequences of our actions. But just because our wills are weak doesn't mean they don't exist. Sometimes we use reason to decide not only what is best for us but also what is best for others, and not just relatives and friends, but all our fellow humans, and even other living things. We reason, and act, morally.

Free will is not a binary property, which you either have or lack. It varies in intensity. My teenage daughter and son have more free will—more choices to consider and select from—than they did when they were infants. I have (on my good days) more free will than adults my age suffering from Alzheimer's disease, obsessive-compulsive disorder, or psychopathy. Free will is a function of our social, cultural, economic, and political milieu as well as our biology. Try telling prisoners in Guantanamo, Tibetans living under Chinese rule, or Sudanese women fleeing ruthless militants that free will does not exist. "Let's change places," they might say, "since you have nothing to lose."

My view of free will resembles the position of the philosopher Daniel Dennett. In his 2003 book *Freedom Evolves*, Dennett lays out a sensible view of free will. He notes, first, that free will is "not what tradition declares it to be: a God-like power to exempt oneself from the causal fabric of the physical world." Free will, he argues, is an emergent property of the brain, like consciousness, that allows us to perceive, mull over, and act upon choices; in fact, choice, or even freedom, are reasonable synonyms for free will.

Dennett calls free will "an evolved creation of human activity and beliefs," which humanity acquired recently as a consequence of language and culture as well as consciousness. Our free will grows along with our knowledge, material well-being, and political freedom. Dennett's most subtle, profound point is that free will is both an "objective phenomenon" and dependent on our belief in and perception of it. In other words, as we believe we have more free will, freedom, and choices, we actually do have more.

A recent experiment confirms Dennett's claim that belief in free will has measurable consequences. The psychologists Kathleen Vohs and Jonathan Schooler asked subjects to read a passage by Crick that casts doubt on free will. Crick writes that "although we appear to have free will, in fact, our choices have already been predetermined for us and we cannot change that." Subjects who read this passage were more likely to cheat on a test than control subjects who read a passage about brain science that did not mention free will. Mere exposure to the idea that we are not really responsible for our actions, it seems, makes us less moral. These results, the researchers conclude, "point to a significant value in believing that free will exists."

Belief in free will underpins all our ethics and morality. It forces us to take responsibility for ourselves rather than consigning our fate to genes or divine planning. Choices, freely made, are what make life meaningful. Denying free will means denying that our conscious, psychological deliberations influence our actions. Our lives hinge on choices, over which we often agonize. Should I major in mechanical engineering or music? Keep going to church to please my parents? Vote for Barack Obama or his opponent? Ask my girlfriend to marry me? Enlist in the Army or the Peace Corps? Bomb Qaddafi or negotiate with him? Free will works better than any other single criterion for gauging or explaining the vitality of a life or a society. And if we don't believe we're free, we will be less free.

CHARMY'S HOPE

To help them appreciate the importance of free will, I occasionally ask my students whether they would rather live today or in the Stone Age, prior to civilization. Although some students are enticed by the imagined simplicity of hunter-gatherer life, most choose the present. They express appreciation for iPhones, cars, jets, television, the internet, beds, microwave ovens, take-out pizza—as well as the comfort and security of life in a first-world country. A few provide the answer I am really looking for. "In today's world anyone can try to do anything they want," one student, Tim, wrote a while back. "It is this freedom of choice that is the reason why I would rather live in modern times than in the Paleolithic era."

"Yes!" I scribbled in the margin of Tim's paper. Our Paleolithic ancestors had little or no choice when it came to where, how, or with whom they lived. The very notion of choice would have been foreign to them. My students—and my two children—have degrees of freedom that our ancestors could not have imagined. With hard work and a little luck, young people today can become video-game designers, brain surgeons, organic farmers, pastry chefs, even science journalists. They can be gay, straight, or bisexual, married or single. They can have three kids, or no kids. They can worship God, Allah, Mother Nature, or the Almighty Dollar.

Many people in this country and around the world—far too many, and these are no doubt tough economic times—still don't have meaningful choices. But civilization keeps giving more of us more freedom, including the freedom to help those oppressed by poverty, tyranny, racism, sexism, ignorance, and war. I tell my students, most of whom are engineering majors, that they can make the world a better place by designing more efficient photovoltaic cells or portable water purification systems for people in third-world countries. They can also speak out against this nation's exorbitant military budget, arms sales to other nations, and involvement in wars overseas. They can vote or volunteer for or *become* politicians who make ending war a priority.

The end of war, I tell my students, means the end of one especially destructive, stupid, immoral form of conflict—not all forms. We will still get angry with each other and bicker over the usual things: politics, money, morality, ideology, religion, sex, love. But ending war and even the threat of war between nations will transform the world in countless ways.

I've persuaded some of my students to share my optimism. One was Charmy, a Muslim born and raised in India. She was a biochemistry major and hoped to become a doctor. At the beginning of my "War and Human Nature" class, Charmy was one of my most pessimistic students. She worried that conflicts between haves and have-nots in India, and between Muslims and Hindus, might erupt into large-scale violence. The long-simmering tension between India and Pakistan, she told me, might even trigger a nuclear war.

By the end of the semester, she had apparently changed her mind. Maybe she felt sorry for me, but I doubt it, because throughout the semester she had been brutally blunt. If I said something she found foolish, Charmy rolled her eyes and let me know. In her final paper, she still expressed doubts, reminding me that wars are raging in Afghanistan, Iraq, and elsewhere.

But she saw signs of progress, such as India's offer to help Pakistan after Pakistan was devastated by an earthquake. In her final paper, Charmy explored measures that she thought might reduce the risk of war: finding alternatives to fossil fuels, improving education, supporting democracy, bolstering U.N. peace-keeping efforts, and promoting international exchange programs (like the one that brought her to my school). Charmy emphasized that none of these steps guarantees peace. If people want to wage war, she said, they will always have plenty of excuses to do so.

But at the end of her essay, Charmy allowed herself to dream a little. "Imagine a future in which the children ask their mothers, 'What were wars?' Every child, man and woman will have enough to eat, to cover themselves, access to a school, and a clean and beautiful environment, regardless of their religion or nationality. Just imagine other infinite possibilities available to humans with their resources, their intellect, and most importantly, their creativity!"

The hope of the young gives me hope.

A Brief Prehistory of Violence

3,000,000 YA (YEARS AGO): KILLER APEMEN?

The anthropologist Raymond Dart asserted that holes in *Australopithecus* skulls were caused by other Australopithecenes 3 million years ago. Popularizations of Dart's work, which depicted our ancestors as "killer apes," allegedly inspired the "Dawn of Man" scene of the 1968 film *2001: A Space Odyssey*, in which one ape man beats another to death with a bone. The marks studied by Dart are now attributed to predators and natural causes.

2,600,000 YA: STONE CHOPPERS, AXES

The oldest known stone tools are choppers found in Ethiopia in conjunction with butchered bones of animals that lived 2,600,000 years ago. Stone axes have been dated to 1,700,000 years ago. The first stone tools mark the beginning of the Paleolithic Era, or "Old Stone Age," during which our ancestors lived as nomadic hunter-gatherers. The era lasted until humans invented agriculture and began living in permanent settlements less than 12,000 years ago.

780,000 YA: BUTCHERED BONES

Homo erectus bones found in Atapuerca Dolina, Spain, show signs of having been butchered. Similar marks have been found on 600,000-year-old hominid bones from Ethiopia and more recent Neanderthal bones in France and elsewhere. "Defleshing," anthropologist Tim White says, "cannot be considered evidence" for lethal group violence. Marks are more likely evidence of ritualistic treatment of the dead or of starvation-driven cannibalism, White says.

400,000 YA: SPEARS

The oldest known spears, found in a mine in Germany and estimated to be 400,000 years old, had heat-hardened wooden tips. Spears tipped with stone points do not appear in the archaeological record until 50,000 years ago. Spears are not unique to humans: chimpanzees have been observed hunting bush babies with sharp sticks.

200,000 YA: *HOMO SAPIENS* APPEARS

50,000 YA: NEANDERTHAL VIOLENCE?

Grooves on the ribs of a 50,000-year-old Neanderthal skeleton found in Iraq's Shanidar cave suggest that he was pierced by a sharp object. Partial healing indicates that he lived for several weeks before dying. The wound may have resulted from a fight with another human. But these and other injuries found on skeletons of Neanderthals and *Homo sapiens* during the Stone Age, says the anthropologist Erik Trinkaus, probably resulted from "hunting large animals who object to being speared."

40,000 YA: ATLATLS (SPEAR-THROWERS)

The atlatl, a device for hurling spears with much greater force than the unaided arm, first appeared in the Old World (Africa, Asia, and Europe) 40,000 years ago and in the New World 8,500 years ago.

25,000 YA: BOOMERANGS

Although usually associated with Australia, boomerangs were also widely used by prehistoric people in Europe and Africa. The earliest known boomerang, found in a cave in Poland and estimated to be 25,000 years old, was carved from a mammoth tusk.

22,000 YA: BOWS AND ARROWS

Although the oldest arrowheads are more than 20,000 years old, bows and arrows are thought to have become widespread in the Old World 15,000 years ago and in the New World 1,500 years ago.

20,000 YA: OLDEST HOMICIDE VICTIM

The oldest skeleton bearing clear-cut signs of lethal human violence—embedded projectile points—was found in the Nile Valley in the Sudan and dated at 20,000 years old. Other famous early victims of violence include "Kennewick Man," an 8,400-year-old skeleton found in Washington State, and "Ötzi the Iceman," who died in the Alps 5,300 years ago. Both skeletons had arrowheads embedded in them and bore other marks of violence. Virtually all anthropologists believe that homicide—as opposed to warfare between groups—has occurred at least occasionally throughout human evolution.

13,000 YA, OLDEST MASS GRAVE

The oldest strong evidence of group violence is a mass grave found in the Nile Valley in northern Sudan. The grave contains fifty-nine skeletons, twenty-four of which bear marks of violence, including embedded stone points. Many anthropologists consider this grave to be evidence of group violence, but some remain skeptical, pointing out that the bodies were apparently killed and buried over an extended period. The victims could have been killed individually, perhaps in executions or ritual sacrifices, rather than warfare.

10,000 YA: HUNTER-GATHERER WARFARE

In northern Australia, rock drawings estimated to be 10,000 years old depict groups of men brandishing boomerangs and spears. These drawings provide strong evidence that at least some nomadic hunter-gatherers had begun to engage in warfare.

10,000 YA: WIDESPREAD WARFARE

The first irrefutable evidence of significant warfare—including fortifications, spear and arrow points, and bones bearing marks of violence—was found in northern Mesopotamia and dated at 10,000 years old. Similar evidence suggests that war arose in the Near East 9,500 years ago, in Turkey 8,000 years ago, in China 7,000 years ago, in Europe 6,500 years ago, in the American Northwest 4,200 years ago, and in the American Southwest 2,000 years ago. Agriculture and permanent settlements had emerged before war in most of these regions, but people in others still lived as hunter-gatherers.

APPENDIX SOURCES:

—"Once Were Cannibals," by Tim White, *Scientific American*, August 2001, online at scribd.com/doc/27015818/Once-Were-Cannibals.

—"The Birth of War," by Brian Ferguson, *Natural History*, July/August 2003, online at andromeda.rutgers.edu/~socant/Birth%20of%20War.pdf.

—"Timeline: Weapons Technology," by Michael Marshall, *New Scientist*, July 7, 2009, online at newscientist.com/article/dn17423-timeline-weapons-technology.html.

—*How War Began*, by Keith Otterbein, Texas A&M University Press, 2004.

—*The Human Potential for Peace*, by Douglas P. Fry, Oxford University Press, 2006.

—Interviews with Tim White, Erik Trinkaus, Brian Ferguson, and Douglas Fry.

ENDNOTES

Introduction: Living in Wartime

13   "We had a great day. We killed a lot of people": "A Nation at War: In the
      Field," by Dexter Filkins, the *New York Times*, March 29, 2003.

14   the show "Radiolab": the show originally aired October 19, 2009, and is
      online at radiolab.org/2009/oct/19/new-baboon.

16   "Only the dead": for a discussion of this quote, often attributed to Plato,
      see this essay by the amateur philosophy scholar Bernard Suzanne, plato-
      dialogues.org/faq/faq008.htm The film *Black Hawk Down* attributes the
      quote to Plato, as does General Douglas MacArthur in a 1962 speech
      at West Point. But according to Suzanne, scholars have not found the
      quote in Plato's writings. It occurs in a book of essays by the British
      philosopher George Santayana, *Soliloquies in England* (Scribners, 1924), p.
      102. After overhearing British veterans exulting at the end of World War
      I, Santayana comments: "Yet the poor fellows think they are safe! They
      think that the war is over! Only the dead have seen the end of war."

16   Obama declared: "War, in one form": the full text of Obama's Nobel
      acceptance speech can be found at nobelprize.org/nobel_prizes/peace/
      laureates/2009/obama-lecture_en.html.

20   The story is straight, unsentimental: "Reassuring Hands: A U.S. Crew's
      Urgent Flight into the Afghan Desert," by C.J. Chivers, the *New York
      Times*, December 19, 2010, p. A8.

20   But consider these incidents: the two incidents are reported in these two
      articles in the *New York Times*: "Afghan Investigators Say U.S. Troops
      Tried to Cover Up Evidence in Botched Raid," by Richard A. Oppel and
      Abdul Waheed Wafa, April 6, 2010, p. A4; and "Study Cites Drone Crew
      In Attack on Afghans," by Christopher Drew, September 11, 2010, p. A8.

21   the trial of Steven Hayes: see "Death Penalty for a Killer of Three in
      Connecticut," by William Glaberson, the *New York Times*, November 9,
      2010.

22   "rapidly rendering war obsolete": I found this quote from Mill in *On the
      Origin of War*, by Donald Kagan, Anchor Books, 1995, p. 2.

22   *The Great Illusion*: Angell's book was originally published in 1909 under

the title *Europe's Optical Illusion.*

23   "We are living through": *No More War!*, by Linus Pauling, 25th
anniversary edition, Dodd, Mead & Co., 1983, p. xiii.

23   "problems of the kind": *ibid.*, p. 229.

23   "there will be no need to republish the book": *ibid*, p. xv.

25   "There is no way": the pacifist and social activist A.J. Muste is credited
with coining this slogan during World War I.

Chapter One: War Is Not Innate

30   "These results," he writes: "The Myth That War Is Intrinsic to Human
Nature Discourages Action for Peace by Young People," by David Adams
and Sarah Bosch, *Essays on Violence*, edited by J. Martin Ramirez *et al,*
Publicaciones de la Universidad de Sevilla, Seville, 1987, p. 134.

30   The Seville Statement: UNESCO has posted the statement and a list
of the original signers at portal.unesco.org/education/en/ev.php-URL_
ID=3247&URL_DO=DO_TOPIC&URL_SECTION=201.html.

31   The statement has been endorsed: David Adams lists endorsers of the
Seville Statement at culture-of-peace.info/vita/2011/seville2011.pdf.

32   Hilali Matama, a researcher at Gombe: this incident is recounted in
Demonic Males, by Richard Wrangham and Dale Peterson, Houghton
Mifflin, 1996.

33   "Chimpanzee-like violence," he writes: Wrangham, *ibid.*, p. 63.

33   Human males "enjoy the opportunity": unless otherwise indicated,
Wrangham's quotes are from interviews that I conducted with him by
phone on May 10, 2007, and May 18, 2009 (this latter interview was posted
on Bloggingheads.tv on May 23, 2009, bloggingheads.tv/diavlogs/19925).

33   "Yay, our side won!": Wrangham made this remark while speaking
at "The Evolution of Human Aggression," a conference held at the
University of Utah in Salt Lake City, February 25-27, 2009.

34   "In the real world": Wrangham, *Demonic Males*, p. 241.

34   Hillary Clinton is reportedly a fan: Francis Fukuyama calls *Demonic
Males* "a favorite book" of Hillary Clinton in his essay "Women and the

Evolution of World Politics," *Foreign Affairs*, vol. 77, no. 5, 1998, pp. 24-40.

34   "feminine" political leaders: *ibid.*

35   *Sex and War*, by Malcolm Potts and Thomas Hayden, BenBella Books, Dallas, Texas, 2008.

35   *The Most Dangerous Animal*, by David Livingston Smith, St. Martin's Press, 2007.

35   "Chimpicide," he writes: *The Blank Slate*, by Steven Pinker, Viking, 2002, p. 316.

35   "the median death rate from intergroup aggression": "Killer Species," by Richard Wrangham, *Daedalus*, vol. 133, no. 4, Fall 2004, pp. 25-35.

36   only twelve deaths from lethal intergroup aggression: "Are Humans Inherently Killers?" by Robert Sussman and Joshua Marshack, *Global Nonkilling Working Papers*, # 1, 2010, nonkilling.org/pdf/wp1.pdf.

36   These observations are based on 215 total researcher-years: *ibid.*

36   "five o'clock news": Sussman made this remark at "Man the Hunted," a conference that he organized at Washington University in St. Louis, March 12-24, 2009.

36   coalitionary killings are "certainly rare": "Chimpanzee Violence Is a Serious Topic," Richard Wrangham, *Global Nonkilling Working Papers*, # 1, 2010, nonkilling.org/pdf/wp1.pdf.

37   "was having a marked effect": this Goodall quote is from Sussman and Marshack, *op. cit.*, p. 22.

37   "related to population stress": email communication, Ian Tattersall.

37   "significant cultural variation": "Cultures in chimpanzees," A. Whiten *et al* (co-authors include Jane Goodall and Richard Wrangham), *Nature*, vol. 399, June 17, 1999, pp. 682-685.

38   "enormous variation in the rates": Wrangham, *Global Nonkilling Working Papers*, p. 39.

38   "the roles of specialized military units": *ibid.*, p. 38.

38   I visited Frans de Waal: I interviewed de Waal at the Yerkes Primate Research Center on June 12, 2007. I also communicated with him by

email several times thereafter.

38   evidence of chimpanzees' generosity: these and other incidents can be
       found in de Waal's *The Age of Empathy*, Three Rivers Press, 2009.

40   "The frontal orientation of the bonobo vulva": "Bonobo Sex and Society,"
       by Frans de Waal, *Scientific American*, March, 1995, pp. 82-88.

40   "females often rush to the other side": *ibid*.

40   Some critics charge: see for example "Swingers," by Ian Parker, the *New
       Yorker*, July 30, 2007, pp. 49-61.

40   "exactly, equally relevant": interview, de Waal, June 12, 2007.

41   *Ardipithecus ramidus* "reveals that the early: "Reexamining Human Origins
       in Light of Ardipithecus ramidus," by C. Owen Lovejoy, *Science*, vol. 326,
       October 2, 2009. For another take on the significance of Ardi, see also "Our
       Kinder, Gentler Ancestors," by Frans de Waal, the *Wall Street Journal*, October
       3, 2009.

41   "tectonic shift": email communication, Owen Lovejoy.

42   The killer ape theory was discredited: the story of Dart's work is told
       in *Beyond War*, by Douglas Fry, Oxford University Press, 2007. For a
       discussion of the influence of Dart and Robert Ardrey on Stanley Kubrick
       and Arthur C. Clark, the creators of the novel and film versions of *2001*,
       see also users.muohio.edu/erlichrd/350/odyssey.php.

42   "an old way of thinking": interview, de Waal, June 12, 2007.

42   adolescent rhesus and stump-tailed macaques: "Modification of
       Reconciliation Behavior through Social Experience," by Frans de Waal and
       Denise Johanowicz, *Child Development*, 1993, vol. 64, pp. 897-908.

43   "they would destroy the world in a week": *On Human Nature*, by Edward O.
       Wilson, Harvard University Press, 1978, p. 104.

44   "nearly as unprecedented as baboons sprouting wings": "A Natural
       History of Peace," by Robert Sapolsky, *Foreign Affairs*, January/February
       2006.

44   "Forest Troop's low aggression": *ibid*.

45   "I looked up and gasped": *Yanomamö: The Fierce People*, by Napoleon
       Chagnon, Holt, Rinehart and Winston, 1968, p. 5.

46   often attributed to Rousseau: see the Wikipedia entry on "Noble Savage" (en.wikipedia.org/wiki/Noble_savage#Erroneous_identification_of_ Rousseau_with_the_noble_savage), which states that Rousseau never used the phrase "noble savage" and was not as anti-civilization as he is often said to be.

46   In 1988, Chagnon made headlines again: "Life Histories, Blood Revenge, and Warfare in a Tribal Population," *Science*, February 26, 1988, pp. 985-992.

46   "wimps": Chagnon used this term when I interviewed him by telephone in 1988.

46   Critics have accused Chagnon: the most serious critique of Chagnon can be found in *Darkness in El Dorado*, by Patrick Tierney, Norton, 2000. I gave the book a positive review in the *New York Times Book Review*, November 12, 2000, p. 6, but many scientists savagely criticized the book. Wikipedia, as of 2011, has a balanced assessment of Chagnon's controversial career: en.wikipedia.org/wiki/Napoleon_Chagnon.

47   I wrote a positive account: "The Violent Yanomamö," *Scientific American*, March, 1988, pp. 17-18.

48   "whose way of life had remained unchanged": this quote is from the publisher's description of *The Harmless People*, by Elizabeth Marshall Thomas, Vintage, 1989 (originally published in 1959). For a report on another modern-day hunter-gatherer group, see "The Hadza," by Michael Finkel, *National Geographic*, December 2009. The author states flatly: "The Hadza do not engage in warfare" (ngm.nationalgeographic. com/2009/12/hadza/finkel-text).

49   in the nineteenth century the !Kung raided: *War Before Civilization*, by Lawrence Keeley, Oxford University Press, 1996, p. 29.

50   Jebel Sahaba: for a discussion of the Jebel Sahaba site, see Keeley, *op. cit.*, p. 37, and Fry, *op. cit.*, p. 53. Fry notes that "homicides and executions" could account for the violent deaths at Jebel Sahaba, which also apparently occurred over several generations rather than in one incident.

50   The oldest known homicide victim: see Keeley, *op. cit.*, p. 37.

50   Most of the other evidence for warfare: for good overviews of the evidence of early warfare, see Keeley and Fry, *ops. cit.*; *How War Began*, by Keith

Otterbein, Texas A&M Press, 2004; and "The Birth of War," by Brian Ferguson, *Natural History*, July/August 2003 (online at andromeda. rutgers.edu/~socant/Birth%20of%20War.pdf).

50 "You find a lot of evidence of bumps": email interview, Trinkhaus, 2010. Keeley, *op. cit.*, p. 36, also acknowledges that "many of the traumas found on early hominid skeletons have been proved by subsequent investigation to have had non-homicidal causes or cannot be distinguished from accidental traumas of a similar character."

51 "cannot be considered evidence": email interview, Tim White.

51 "we can be fairly certain that lethal aggression": this and other quotes in this chapter are from a 2011 email interview with Sarah Blaffer Hrdy. I also spoke to Hrdy at "The Evolution of Human Aggression," held at the University of Utah in Salt Lake City, February 25-27, 2009.

52 clear-cut relics of other complex cultural behaviors: for an overview of evidence for art and other complex behaviors, see *The Art Instinct*, by Denis Dutton, Bloomsbury, 2009; *Catching Fire*, by Richard Wrangham, Basic Books, 2009; *Mothers and Others*, by Sarah Blaffer Hrdy, Belknap, 2009; and *The Prehistory of the Mind*, by Steven Mithen, Thames and Hudson, 1996.

52 capacity for language is innate: see *The Language Instinct*, by Steven Pinker, Harper Perennial, 1994.

52 "The Irrelevance of Biology": Keeley, *op. cit.*, pp. 158-159.

53 In his interviews with me, he consistently denied: I interviewed Chagnon by phone in 1988 and by phone and in person during and after the annual meeting of the Human Behavior and Evolution Society in Santa Barbara, June 28-July 2, 1995.

53 Many Yanomamö warriors have confessed: *Yanomamö: The Last Days of Eden*, by Napoleon Chagnon, Harcourt Brace Jovanovich, 1992, p. xvi.

53 "Steve Gould and I": phone interview, Chagnon, 1995.

53 more than 99 percent, according to one estimate: *War and Gender*, by Joshua Goldstein, Cambridge University Press, 2001, p. 10.

Chapter Two: You Can't Blame It All on a Few Bad Apples

56   "War is a lot of things": *War*, by Sebastian Junger, Twelve, 2010, p. 144. For a radically different view of war, read *With the Old Breed*, by Eugene Sledge, Presidio Press, 1981. Sledge, a Marine infantryman during World War II, gives an excruciatingly vivid grunt's description of vicious battles in the Pacific between Americans and Japanese. Sledge captures the decency, courage, and camaraderie of men in war, but also the savagery, randomness, terror, waste, filth. After weeks of nonstop combat, the Americans hated the Japanese. Sledge and his buddies occasionally found the corpses of American soldiers with their genitals cut off and stuffed in their mouths. Marines would never do such a thing, Sledge says. But one soldier in his troop sliced open the cheeks of a still-living Japanese soldier to more easily pry out his gold fillings. An American officer cheerfully urinated into the mouths of dead Japanese. "War is brutish, inglorious and a terrible waste," Sledge writes. But "until the millennium arrives and countries cease trying to enslave others, it will be necessary to accept one's responsibility and to be willing to make sacrifices for one's country."

56   "moral basis of the war": Junger, *pp. cit.*, p. 25.

56   "The politically incorrect truth": "Sebastian Junger Bleeds for Restrepo," by Rob Nelson, the *Village Voice*, June 15, 2010, villagevoice.com/content/printVersion/1864862.

56   Junger cites the work of Wrangham: Junger, *op. cit.*, p. 281.

57   "Indeed, it is not necessary": *An Intimate History of Killing*, by Joanna Bourke, Basic Books, 1999, p. xvii.

57   "immune from this intoxication": *ibid.*, p. 19.

57   "great and seductive beauty": *ibid.*, pp. 1-2.

58   soldiers involuntarily urinate or defecate: *On Combat*, by Dave Grossman, PPCT Research Publications, 2004, pp. 9-10.

58   more than half a million soldiers: *On Killing*, by Dave Grossman, Little Brown, 1996, p. 43.

58   psychiatrists Roy Swank and Walter Marchand: For a discussion of Swank and Marchand's 1946 study, see Grossman, *On Killing*, pp. 43-44.

59   "The average and normally healthy individual": *ibid.*, p. 1.

59   Critics have questioned whether Marshall: *ibid.*, p. xv. (See also the Wikipedia entry on Marshall, which reports on the controversies surrounding his work: en.wikipedia.org/wiki/S.L.A._Marshall.)

59   A survey of World War II fighter pilots: *ibid.*, p. 30.

59   experiment carried out by the Prussian Army: *ibid.*, p. 19.

59   hundreds of Prussian soldiers: *ibid.*, pp. 10-11.

59   French troops discharged 48,000 rounds: *ibid.*, p. 12

60   "powerful, innate human resistance": *ibid.*, p. xxix.

60   "With the proper conditioning": *ibid.*, p. 4.

60   "kill, kill, kill": *ibid.*, p. 251.

60   firing rates among infantrymen rose: *ibid.*, p. 35.

60   As many as 25 percent: *ibid.*, p. 247.

60   9 percent of all Vietnam veterans still suffer: "The psychological risks of Vietnam for U.S. veterans," by B.P. Dohrenwend *et al, Science*, August 18, 2006, p. 979.

61   RAND... reported in 2008: RAND's 2008 report, "Invisible Wounds of War Project," can be found online at rand.org/multi/military/veterans.html.

61   it "can give us purpose, meaning": *War Is a Force That Gives Us Meaning*, by Chris Hedges, Anchor Books, 2002, p. 3.

62   "part of the human condition": *ibid.*, p. 16.

62   "War is brutal and impersonal": "The Pictures of War You Aren't Supposed to See," by Chris Hedges, *Truthdig*, January 4, 2010, online at truthdig.com/report/item/the_pictures_of_war_you_arent_supposed_to_see_20100104.

62   "the capacity for levelheaded participation in combat": Grossman, *op. cit.*, p. 184.

63   "aggressive psychopathic personalities": *ibid.*, p. 44.

63   3 percent of all males show symptoms of antisocial personality disorder: *DSM-IV*, American Psychiatric Association, 1994, p. 648.

63   Psychopaths "lie and manipulate": "Inside the Mind of a Psychopath," by Kent Kiehl and Joshua Buckholtz, *Scientific American Mind*, September 2010.

64   "insights into others' vulnerabilities": ibid.

64   The researchers estimated the heritability of psychopathy: "Evidence for
      substantial genetic risk for psychopathy in 7-year-olds," by Robert Plomin
      et al, Journal of Child Psychology and Psychiatry, vol. 46, no. 6, 2005, pp. 592-
      597 (online at socialbehavior.uzh.ch/teaching/semsocialneurosciencews07/
      Vidingetal_2005JCPP.pdf).

65   2 percent of Hutu males: I found this statistic in "Why Isn't There More
      Violence?" by John Mueller, *Security Studies*, vol. 13, no. 3, Spring 2004, p.
      200.

65   small percentages of men... are responsible: *Final Solution*, by Benjamin
      Valentino, Cornell University Press, 2004.

65   Barbara Oakley argues: *Evil Genes*, by Barbara Oakley, Prometheus Books,
      2007.

65   "the greatest of all experiences": I found this Hitler quote in *A History of
      Warfare*, by John Keegan, Alfred A. Knopf, 1993, p. 366.

65   "terribly and terrifyingly normal": *Eichmann in Jerusalem*, by Hannah
      Arendt, Penguin, 1995, p. 276.

66   U.S. homicide rates: see for example this United Nations Office of Drugs
      and Crime report on 2004 international homicide rates at unodc.org/
      documents/data-and-analysis/IHS-rates-05012009.pdf.

67   In 1993, the National Academy of Sciences concluded: *Understanding and
      Preventing Violence*, National Academy Press, 1993. See also Wikipedia's
      excellent overview, en.wikipedia.org/wiki/XYY_syndrome.

67   British researchers reported links: "Role of genotype in the cycle of
      violence in maltreated children," by Avshalom Caspi *et al*, *Science*,
      August 2, 2002, pp. 851-854.

67   followup studies failed to confirm: "Monoamine oxidase A (MAOA)
      and antisocial behaviors in the presence of childhood and adolescent
      maltreatment," by Brett Haberstick *et al*, *American Journal of Medical
      Genetics*, May 5, 2005; and "Interaction between MAO-A genotype and
      maltreatment in the risk for conduct disorder," by S.E. Young *et al*,
      American Journal of Psychiatry, vol. 163, no. 6, 2006, pp. 951-953.

67   touting what was now being called "the warrior gene": the oldest use

I have found of the term "warrior gene" to describe the MAO-A allele
is "Tracking the Evolutionary History of a 'Warrior Gene,'" by Ann
Gibbons, *Science*, May 7, 2004, p. 818.

68   "It is well recognized": "Monoamine oxidase, addiction, and the 'warrior'
gene hypothesis," by Rod Lea and Geoffrey Chambers, *Journal of the New
Zealand Medical Association*, March 2, 2007.

68   media hailed an experiment: the scientific report on the experiment is
"Monoamine oxidase A gene (MAOA) predicts behavioral aggression
following provocation," *Proceedings of the National Academy of
Sciences*, by Rose McDermott *et al*, January 23, 2009, online at pnas.
org/content/106/7/2118.abstract. The ABC News report on the
research, titled "One-in-three men have violence gene," can be found
online at abcnews.go.com/Nightline/warrior-gene-tied-violence/
story?id=12422661&page=1, and the National Geographic broadcast,
titled "Born to Rage?", is online at channel.nationalgeographic.com/series/
explorer/4833/Overview.

70   "Almost everyone, including the Yanomamö": *Yanomamö: The Last Days of
Eden*, by Napoleon Chagnon, Harcourt Brace Jovanovich, 1992, p. xvi.

71   "a less cruel, happier, and better man": *Physical Control of the Mind: Toward
a Psychocivilized Society*, by Jose Delgado, Harper Colophon, 1969, p. 232.
Delgado also writes: "In some old plantations slaves… were probably
happier than some of the free blacks in modern ghettos. In several
dictatorial countries the general population is skillful, productive, well
behaved and perhaps as happy as those in more democratic societies. It is
doubtful, however, that slavery or dictatorship should be our models." See
also my profile of Delgado and other early brain-chip researchers, "The
Forgotten Era of Brain Chips," *Scientific American*, October 2005.

72   The Nazis gave eugenics a bad name: the historian Daniel Kevles provides a
gripping history of eugenics in *In the Name of Eugenics*, Alfred A. Knopf, 1985.

72   the hormone oxytocin: for an overview of oxytocin, see "Depth of the
Kindness Hormone Appears to Know Some Bounds," by Nicholas Wade,
the *New York Times*, January 10, 2011, online at nytimes.com/2011/01/11/
science/11hormone.html.

72   "The Moral Equivalent of War": James' essay can be found online at
constitution.org/wj/meow.htm.

72   "sporting contests": *On Aggression*, by Konrad Lorenz, Harcourt, Brace, 1966, p. 282.

72   propensity for war and their fondness for sports: see "War, Sports and Aggression: An Empirical Test of Two Rival Theories," by Richard Sipes, *American Anthropologist*, vol. 75, no. 1, February, 1973, online at onlinelibrary.wiley.com/doi/10.1525/aa.1973.75.1.02a00040/abstract. Sipes suggests that, if anything, sports and war are positively correlated. He notes that "where we find warlike behavior we typically find combative sports, and where war is relatively rare combative sports tend to be absent."

73   war sexually arousing: war has always been associated with high levels of rape and consensual sex. "There is in wartime a nearly universal preoccupation with sexual liaisons," writes Chris Hedges, *op. cit.*, p. 100. In his book *What Every Person Should Know About War*, Free Press, 2003, p. 33, Hedges cites a survey which found that American soldiers stationed in Europe during World War II had sex with women, on average, during their last year of service. Grossman, *On Killing, op. cit.*, pp. 270-271, offers a Darwinian explanation of the correlation between sexual arousal and violence: "There might be a tendency for a female to be drawn to an alpha male who can protect her, and there might be a tendency for the male to spread the genes around in the face of anxiety and sudden death."

73   women can make also ferocious warriors: the material on the Dahomey female warriors, the Russian "Battalion of Death," and the white-feather campaign is from *War and Gender*, by Joshua Goldstein, Cambridge University Press, 2001.

74   "the men knew no shame": *ibid.*, p. 75.

74   "We would be lucky": *ibid.*, p. 131.

Chapter Three: Does Resource Scarcity Make Us Fight?
(No, Not Necessarily)

77   Entering the lobby: I interviewed Steven LeBlanc at the Peabody Museum May 18, 2007, as well as over the phone and by email before and after that date.

78   "a common and almost universal human behavior": *Constant Battles*, by

Steven LeBlanc and Katherine Register, St. Martin's Press, 2003, p. 8.

78   "Since the beginning of time": *ibid.*, p. xiv.

79   "melancholy" theory: Thomas Malthus first published his "Essay on the Principle of Population" in 1798. See Wikipedia's entry on Malthus: en.wikipedia.org/wiki/Thomas_Robert_Malthus.

79   "the competition over scarce resources": *War in Human Civilization*, by Azar Gat, Oxford University Press, 2006, p. 668.

80   "more rather than less likely": I found this quote in *Eaarth*, by Bill McKibben, Times Books, 2010, p. 82.

80   "civilization itself could distintegrate": "Could Food Shortages Bring Down Civilization?" by Lester Brown, *Scientific American*, May 2009, p. 50.

81   One Defense Department study concluded": see "Pentagon Says Global Warming Is a Critical National Security Issue," by David Stipp, *Fortune*, January 26, 2004, online at money.cnn.com/magazines/fortune/fortune_archive/2004/02/09/360120/index.htm.

82   "circumscription theory": "A Theory of the Origin of the State," by Robert Carneiro, *Science*, August 21, 1970, pp. 733-738. For a recent overview of circumscription theory, see the Wikipedia entry, en.wikipedia.org/wiki/Carneiro%27s_Circumscription_Theory.

82   "Force, and not enlightened self-interest": Carneiro, *op. cit.*, p. 734.

83   fighting among the Chumash escalated: "Patterns of Violence in Prehistoric Hunter-gatherer Societies of Coastal Southern California," by Patricia Lambert, chapter four in *Troubled Times: Violence and Warfare in the Past*, edited by Debra Martin and David Frayer, Gordon and Breach, 1997, pp. 77-109.

83   Norse culture in Greenland: Jared Diamond provides a gripping account of the rise and fall of the Norse Greenland colony in his book *Collapse*, Viking, 2005.

84   "For this land which you now inhabit": I found this translation of Pope Urban's proclamation at cliojournal.wikispaces.com/Pope+Urban+and+the+First+Crusade.

85   Abü Hureyra: the anthropologist Keith Otterbein discusses the significance of Abu Hureyra in *How War Began*, Texas A&M University

Press, 2004 pp. 222-223. He calls Abü Hureyra a "wonderful example" of a society that "can survive for thousands of years without warfare." See also "The Eloquent Bones of Abu Hureya," by T. Molleson, *Scientific American*, August 1994; and Keeley, *War Before Civilization*, p. 120, where he cites examples of early agricultural communities in the Near East that experienced large population growth with "no indications of warfare at all"; conversely, widely dispersed populations of hunter-gatherers in central Europe "seem to have been quite violent." Keeley concludes that "the association between human density and the intensity of warfare was as complex or weak in prehistory as in the ethnographic record."

85   Ur and Uruk... thrived for centuries: see *A History of Warfare*, by John Keegan, Vintage Books, 1993, p. 128. Otterbein, *op. cit.*, also claims that evidence of warfare appears late in some early agricultural civilizations.

85   "War is bad and nobody likes it": Keeley, *op cit.*, p. 145.

85   "If one insists on a narrow cause-effect relationship": *Yanomamö: The Last Days of Eden*, by Napoleon Chagnon, Harcourt Brace Jovanovich, 1992. p. 113.

86   Human Relations Area Files: see the HRAF website, yale.edu/hraf.

86   I interviewed them in their offices: I interviewed the Embers in New Haven on July 13, 2004.

86   186 cultures from all over the world: the Embers summarize their findings in papers such as "Violence in the Ethnographic Record," a chapter in *Troubled Times: Violence and Warfare in the Past*, edited by Debra Martin and David Frayer, Gordon and Breach, 1997; and "Making the world more peaceful," an essay in *Prevention and Control of Aggression and the Impact on its Victims*, edited by M. Martinez, Kluwer Academic/Plenum Publishers, 2001.

87   "Societies with only the threat of disasters": "Resource Unpredictability, Mistrust, and War," *Journal of Conflict Resolution*, vol. 36, no. 2, June 1992, p. 256, online at jcr.sagepub.com/content/36/2/242. For a list of the cultures included in the Embers' study, see en.wikipedia.org/wiki/Standard_cross-cultural_sample. For an interesting discussion of the link between fear—and especially fear of death—and social behavior, see this Wikipedia entry on terror-management theory: en.wikipedia.org/wiki/Terror_management_theory. The theory holds that societies become more

distrustful, authoritarian, ideologically rigid, and warlike when citizens are reminded of their mortality.

88   Thomas Homer-Dixon: see his book *The Upside of Down*, Island Press, 2006. For another excellent discussion of the link between resource scarcity and war, see Diamond, *op. cit.*

89   Average standards of living remained stagnant: the data in this section on historical changes in income, the surge of wealth caused by the industrial revolution, and the success of the "Green Revolution" come from two books by the economist Jeffrey Sachs: *The End of Poverty*, Penguin, 2007; and *Common Wealth*, Penguin, 2008.

89   survive on less than $1.25 a day: see Sachs, *Common Wealth*, and this website for the United Nations Millennium Development Goals: un.org/millenniumgoals.

91   3 million Indians starved to death: *Churchill's Secret War*, by Madhusree Mukerjee, Basic Books, 2010.

91   Richardson spent his early career: a brief biography of Richardson is included in his posthumous book *The Statistics of Deadly Quarrels*, edited by Quincy Wright and C.C. Lienau, Boxwood Press, 1960.

92   "rich and poor were usually intermingled": *ibid.*, p. 205.

93   29 percent of the 244 causes were economic: *ibid.*, p. 210.

94   "radically different national homicide rates": "Income inequality and homicide rates in Canada and the United States," by Martin Daly, Margo Wilson, and Shawn Vasdev, *Canadian Journal of Criminology*, April 2001, pp. 219-236, online at psych.mcmaster.ca/dalywilson/iiahr2001.pdf.

94   less evidence linking economic inequality to homicides: "Income inequality, poverty, and homicide across nations," by Paul-Philippe Pare and Richard Felson, *American Society of Criminology*, October/November 2006.

94   "capitalism with a human face": Sachs, *The End of Poverty*, pp. 357-358. For critiques of humanitarian aid, see *Dead Aid*, by Dambisa Moyo, Farrar, Straus, and Giroux, 2009; and *The Crisis Caravan*, by Linda Polman, Metropolitan Books, 2010. Moyo is an investment banker raised in Zambia, and Polman is a Dutch journalist. Polman's critique is especially harsh. She charges that aid to Africa—including funds, food,

medical supplies, and other items funneled into war-wracked regions like Darfur—ends up exacerbating rather than relieving violence and suffering. Militants steal aid or demand payment from aid workers, Polman asserts, and even commit atrocities—such as cutting arms and feet off civilians—to attract more international attention and hence aid.

95   the government has forced thousands: my friend and former *Scientific American* colleague Madhusree Mukerjee, author of the aforementioned book *Churchill's Secret War*, has reported on abuses of multinational mining companies perpetrated in India and elsewhere in the name of globalization. See for example her articles "Sludgy Secrets of the Aluminum Companies," *Philadelphia Inquirer*, October 15, 2010, online at articles.philly.com/2010-10-15/news/24983259_1_aluminum-smelter-aluminum-companies-bauxite; and "Dancing Around the Flame," *Dissent*, March 11, 2011, dissentmagazine.org/online.php?id=459.

95   He cites… the Pentagon report: McKibben, *op. cit.*, p. 85. McKibben also writes, p. 82, that "conflict seems as likely as cooperation" if the U.S. and other nations do not immediately cut back on fossil-fuel consumption.

97   "naturalist"… "materialist": Keegan, *op. cit.*, p. 79.

97   1957 study by… Sorokin: *Social and Cultural Dynamics*, by Pitirim Sorokin, American Book Co., 1957.

98   "Dreams of an end to war": "The Peace Paradox," by David Bell, the *New York Times Magazine*, February 4, 2007.

Chapter Four: Is War a Cultural Contagion? (Yes)

99   "Mead misled a generation into believing": the Intercollegiate Studies Institute's list of the worst books of the twentieth century can be found online at isi.org/journals/ir/50be.st_worst/50worst.html. For more balanced looks at Mead's career, see en.wikipedia.org/wiki/Margaret_Mead, and "Bursting a South Sea Bubble," by Melvin Konner, *Nature*, March 11, 1999, pp. 117-118. Konner, a prominent anthropologist, says that Mead "got some things wrong," but he praises her contributions to "fighting racist theories, demonstrating the flexibility of sex roles, promoting respect for exotic traditions, challenging the ethnocentrism of psychologists, sociologists and historians, fighting colonialism,

questioning research methods that 'objectify' non-Western people, preserving disappearing cultures and resisting the generalizations of sociobiology." Five years after her death, the anthropologist Derek Freeman published *Margaret Mead and Samoa: The Making and Unmaking of an Anthropological Myth*, Harvard University Press, 1983. Freeman accuses Mead of imposing her sexual fantasies on Samoan culture. Mead's female informants told him that Mead's depictions of their sex lives were inaccurate, in part because they had made up much of what they told her. Mead's defenders in turn accused Freeman of biased, flawed scholarship; he did not take into account the fact that missionaries had converted Mead's former informants to Christianity and had taught them to be ashamed of their youthful sexuality. The anthropologist Melvin Ember, who did fieldwork in Samoa, accuses Freeman of projecting his "aggressive and authoritarian" personality onto his subjects. "If Mead was projecting what she wanted unconsciously to see, and I am not convinced she was," Ember states in "Evidence and Science in Ethnography: Reflections on the Freeman-Mead Controversy," *American Anthropologist*, vol. 87, 1985, pp. 906-910, "it is at least as likely that Freeman is projecting what he wants to see."

100   "blank slates" unconstrained by biology: *The Blank Slate*, by Steven Pinker, Viking, 2002, p. 25. Pinker quotes, disapprovingly, Mead's statement that "human nature is almost unbelievably malleable, responding accurately and contrastingly to contrasting cultural conditions."

100   "human evil is a culturally acquired thing": *Demonic Males*, by Richard Wrangham and Dale Peterson, Houghton Mifflin, 1996, p. 84.

101   "Warfare is Only an Invention—Not a Biological Necessity": Mead's essay was originally published in *Asia*, August, 1940. It can be found online at acme.highpoint.edu/~msetzler/IntlSec/IntlSecReads/MeadeWarCreated. pdf. All the quotes from Mead in this chapter are from this essay, except where indicated.

103   the Waorani and the Semai: these societies are contrasted in "Cultures of War and Peace: A Comparative Study of Waorani and Semai," by Clayton and Carole Robarchek, a chapter in *Aggression and Peacefulness in Humans and Other Primates*, edited by James Silverberg and Patrick Gray, Oxford, 1992, pp. 189-213.

103   sixty-eight times more dense: *ibid.*, p. 208.

104   "We killed, killed, killed": this quote from a Semai scout is from *War Before Civilization*, by Lawrence Keeley, Oxford University Press, 1996, p. 31.

105   war, like an infectious disease: *ibid.*, p. 128, Keeley notes that war among North American Indians often stemmed from "rotten apples that spoiled their regional barrels," that is, belligerent tribes that forced others to fight. Keeley also lists western rotten apples, including "republican Rome, Late Classical Germany, medieval (Viking) Scandinavia, sixteenth-century Spain, seventeenth-century France, revolutionary-Napoleonic France," as well as, more recently, the United States, Germany and Japan. Two other books that explore the contagiousness of war are *The Parable of the Tribes*, by Andrew Bard Schmookler, State University of New York Press, 1995; and *Blood Rites*, by Barbara Ehrenreich, Metropolitan Books, 1997.

105   the desire for revenge: Keeley, *op. cit.*, p. 200.

106   "walling off of boys beyond a certain age": email interview, Sarah Blaffer Hrdy, 2010. See also her book *Mothers and Others*, Belknap, 2009.

106   "The deeds of warriors": Mead, *op. cit.* I recalled Mead's words in 2006 during a trip to Washington, D.C., when I spent one morning jogging past many of the capital's tourist attractions: the White House, ringed with barricades and guard posts, marked and unmarked security vehicles. The Washington Monument, America embodied as a sword. The Lincoln Memorial, where Lincoln broods forever over whether preserving the Union—and even ending slavery—was worth 1 million lives. The half-buried black gash of the Vietnam War Memorial, etched with the names of 58,000 dead American soldiers. And finally, a huge memorial for World War II. The memorial consists of a fountain ringed with columns, one of which bears this inscription from General George Marshall: "WE ARE DETERMINED THAT BEFORE THE SUN SETS ON THIS TERRIBLE STRUGGLE OUR FLAG WILL BE RECOGNIZED THROUGHOUT THE WORLD AS A SYMBOL OF FREEDOM ON THE ONE HAND AND OF OVERWHELMING FORCE ON THE OTHER."

106   Europeans brought their violent customs: A vigorous proponent of the idea that westerners provoked and exacerbated violence among indigenous

people is the anthropologist Brian Ferguson. See his articles "The Birth of War," *Natural History*, July/August 2003, online at andromeda. rutgers.edu/~socant/Birth%20of%20War.pdf); "Tribal Warfare," *Scientific American*, January 1992, andromeda.rutgers.edu/~socant/Tribal%20 Warfare.pdf; and "Blood of the Leviathan," *American Ethnologist*, vol. 17, no. 2, May 1990, online at andromeda.rutgers.edu/~socant/documents/ Blood_of_the_Leviathan.pdf.

107   "They... brought us parrots and balls of cotton and spears and many other things, which they exchanged for the glass beads and hawks' bells": this quote is from *A People's History of the United States*, by Howard Zinn, fourth edition, HarperCollins, 1999, p. 1. My account of the fate of the Wampanoag also comes from Zinn's book.

108   after decades of pondering World War I: Keegan made this confession in "Eliminating the Causes of War," a speech at a conference in Cambridge, England, in 2000, online at pugwash.org/reports/pic/pac256/keegan.htm.

108   "terminated European dominance": *A History of Warfare*, by John Keegan, Vintage Books, 1993, p. 391.

109   "institution of war itself": Keegan, "Eliminating the Causes of War."

109   Simon speculates that extreme altruism: "A Mechanism for Social Selection and Extreme Altruism," by Herbert Simon, *Science*, December 21, 1990. pp. 1665-1669.

110   Milgram's experiments: Milgram first described his experiments in "Behavioral Study of Obedience," *The Journal of Abnormal and Social Psychology*, vol. 67, no. 4, 1963, pp. 371-378. See also Wikipedia's entry for "Milgram experiment," en.wikipedia.org/wiki/Milgram_experiment.

111   "The extreme willingness of adults": "The Perils of Obedience," by Stanley Milgram, *Harper's Magazine*, December 1973, pp. 62-77.

111   "a fatal flaw": *Obedience to Authority*, by Stanley Milgram, Harper and Row, 1974. p. 188.

112   Stanford Prison Experiment: Zimbardo describes the experiment at length in his book *The Lucifer Effect*, Random House, 2007.

113   "rogue" or "rotten" soldiers: *ibid.*, pp. 325-326.

113   "terrifyingly normal": *Eichmann in Jerusalem: A Report on the Banality of*

Evil, by Hannah Arendt, Penguin, 1995, p. 276.

114   My Lai: my account of My Lai comes from *An Intimate History of Killing*, by Joanna Bourke, Basic Books, 1999, pp. 159-163.

114   Calley also cites a biblical precedent: *ibid.*, p. 161.

114   "Under the extreme stress of combat conditions": Zimbardo, *op. cit.*, p. 416-417.

115   When I asked him in an interview: I interviewed Zimbardo in San Francisco on June 14, 2007.

115   "one of the 'fittest' of memes": Ehrenreich, *op. cit.*, p. 234.

115   "must prepare themselves": *ibid.*, p. 241.

116   "Hybrid Warfare": this conference was held May 14-15, 2010. For a list of speakers and topics, see mershoncenter.osu.edu/events/09-10%20events/May10/hybridwarfaremay10.htm.

116   "I don't think there's anything": I interviewed Peter Mansoor at the "Hybrid Warfare" conference on May 15, 2010.

117   James Mattis: in 2005, Mattis was rebuked by the Pentagon for saying in a public talk in San Diego: "You go into Afghanistan, you got guys who slap women around for five years because they didn't wear a veil. You know, guys like that ain't got no manhood left anyway. So it's a hell of a lot of fun to shoot them." See topics.nytimes.com/top/reference/timestopics/people/m/james_n_mattis/index.html.

118   Carneiro suggests that a "world state": Carneiro makes this suggestion in "The Role of Warfare in Political Evolution: Past Results and Future Projections," an essay in *Effects of War on Society*, edited by Giorgio Ausenda, Boydell Press, 2003, pp. 87-102. Carneiro notes that the British poet Alfred Lord Tennyson imagines a united world government in his 1833 poem "Locksley Hall," which reads in part: "the war-drum throbb'd no longer, and the battle-flags were furl'd/In the Parliament of man, the Federation of the world./There the common sense of most shall hold a fretful realm in awe,/And the kindly earth shall slumber, lapped in universal law." Tennyson presents this vision with tragic irony rather than hope.

119   "If we had a world government": I interviewed Pauling in Palo Alto, California, in 1992.

120   correlation between arms possession and violence: see Wikipedia entries
        for rankings of countries by gun ownership (en.wikipedia.org/wiki/
        List_of_countries_by_gun_ownership) and homicide (en.wikipedia.org/
        wiki/List_of_countries_by_intentional_homicide_rate).

120   9.8 homicides for every 100,000: Trends in U.S. homicides and other
        crimes in the twentieth century can be found in the "Historical Data"
        chapter in *Crime and Justice Atlas 2000*, published by the Justice Research
        and Statistics Association, online at jrsa.org/programs/Historical.pdf. See
        also the website of the Bureau of Justice Statistics, bjs.ojp.usdoj.gov.

120   incarceration rates have fallen, too: see "Steady Decline in Major Crime
        Baffles Experts," by Richard Oppel, the *New York Times*, May 23, 2011,
        nytimes.com/2011/05/24/us/24crime.html.

121   "soft-wired... is nearly as resistant": J. David Singer made these remarks
        in "Genetic and Cultural Evolution: Implications for International
        Security Policies," an essay in *Human Nature and Public Policy: An
        Evolutionary Approach*, edited by Albert Somit and Steven Peterson,
        Macmillan, 2003, p. 260.

121   "If we know that it is not inevitable": Mead, *op. cit.*

122   "addicted" to war: *War Is a Force That Gives Us Meaning*, by Chris Hedges,
        Anchor Books, 2002, p. 3.

122   "two-edged sword": *Sex and Temperament in Three Primitive Societies*, by
        Margaret Mead, 1935, William Morrow and Company, p. 289.

123   humans have already invented countless methods: all these methods of
        conflict resolution are from *The Human Potential For Peace*, by Douglas Fry,
        Oxford University Press, 2006.

124   Humans "have a great capacity": *ibid.*, p. xiv.

Chapter Five: Choosing Peace

125   As a boy growing up in Turkey: ghe science journalist David Berreby has
        an excellent account of the life and work of Sherif in *Us and Them*, Little
        Brown, 2005. See also *The Robbers Cave Experiment: Intergroup Conflict and
        Cooperation*, by Muzafer Sherif *et al*, Wesleyan, 1988.

127   Indian emperor Ashoka: see the Wikipedia entry on Ashoka, en.wikipedia. org/wiki/Ashoka.

129   "Once one group adopts it": "Cultures of War and Peace: A Comparative Study of Waorani and Semai," by Clayton and Carole Robarchek, a chapter in *Aggression and Peacefulness in Humans and Other Primates*, edited by James Silverberg and Patrick Gray, Oxford University Press, 1992, p. 197.

129   "unanimously stressed their relief": *ibid.*, 206.

130   "the people themselves": *ibid.*, p. 205.

130   In a 1999 paper: "Global Action to Prevent War," by Randall Forsberg *et al, Boston Review*, February/March 1999, pp. 4-16.

131   interviewed Forsberg in 2003: I interviewed Forsberg in Cambridge, Massachusetts, on September 17, 2003.

131   "change in moral beliefs": Forsberg lays out this view in "Socially-Sanctioned and Non-Sanctioned Violence: On the Role of Moral Beliefs in Causing and Preventing War and Other Forms of Large-Group Violence," a chapter in *Conflict and Violence in the Developing World: Festschrift for Ulrich Albrecht*, Westdeutscher Verlag, 2001, pp. 201-237.

132   "respect for the dignity and worth": *ibid.*, p. 231.

132   initially freed slaves in rebel regions: *A People's History of the United States*, by Howard Zinn, fourth edition, Harper Collins, 1999, pp. 191-192.

132   The U.S. passed child labor laws: most forms of child labor were banned by the Fair Labor Standards Act, passed in 1938. For a brief history of opposition to child labor in the U.S., see en.wikipedia.org/wiki/ Child_labor_laws_in_the_United_States.

133   "because of Hitler": Forsberg made this comment during our 2003 meeting.

133   "on the wane": Forsberg, "Socially-Sanctioned and Non-Sanctioned Violence: On the Role of Moral Beliefs in Causing and Preventing War and Other Forms of Large-Group Violence," p. 230.

133   major armed conflicts... wrack fifteen regions: *SIPRI Yearbook 2011,* Stockholm International Peace Research Institute, 2011. See also sipri.org.

134   AK-47s: the vast majority of war casualties over the past few decades have resulted from so-called "small arms" such as the AK-47, according to the

International Action Network on Small Arms (iansa.org), a London-based group. Small arms, which can be carried and operated by a single person, including a child or small woman, range from pistols and rifles to rocket-launched grenades and shoulder-fired missiles (the latter are sometimes called "light weapons"). There are more than 600 million in circulation globally, according to the IANSA.

135   8 million to over 17 million: *Quiet Cataclysm*, by John Mueller, Harper Collins, 1995, p. 135.

135   from 48,000 to 600,000: "W.H.O. Says Iraq Civilian Death Toll Higher Than Cited," by Lawrence Altman and Richard Oppel, the *New York Times*, January 10, 2008, online at nytimes.com/2008/01/10/world/middleeast/10casualties.html?_r=2&oref=slogin&ref=worldspecial&pagewanted=all.

135   Rummel distinguishes war from "democide": Rummel posts his voluminous annotated statistics on a website, hawaii.edu/powerkills/welcome.html.

135   Leitenberg proposes: "Deaths in Wars and Conflicts in the 20th Century," Cornell University Peace Studies Program, *Occasional Paper #29*, 3rd edition, 2006, online at cissm.umd.edu/papers/files/deathswarsconflictsjune52006.pdf.

136   "Wars grab headlines": "Global Burden of Armed Violence," Geneva Declaration, 2008, p. 26, online at genevadeclaration.org/fileadmin/docs/Global-Burden-of-Armed-Violence-full-report.pdf.

136   490,000, are homicide victims: *ibid.*, p. 3. See also these U.N. reports: unodc.org/unodc/en/data-and-analysis/homicide.html and who.int/violence_injury_prevention/violence/4th_milestones_meeting/4_milestones_meeting_report.pdf. The latter states that about 800,000 people die of suicide each year, as many as die of all other forms of violence combined.

136   "did not lead to the expected increase": this quote is from a press release issued by the Human Security Report Project on December 2, 2010, which can be found online (along with the full text of the "Human Security Report 2009/2010") at hsrgroup.org/press-room/latest-news/latest-news-view/10-12-02/Canadian_Study_Reports_New_Threats_to_Global_Security_but_Reveals_Encouraging_Long-Term_Trends.aspx.

137   fell from seven to four: *SIPRI Yearbook 2011*.

137   bullish assessment for investments: see "Report Offers Optimistic View
        of Africa's Economies," by Celia Dugger, the *New York Times*, June 24,
        2010, p. A8. The McKinsey report, "Lions on the Move," is posted online
        at mckinsey.com/mgi/publications/progress_and_potential_of_african_
        economies/pdfs/MGI_african_economies_full_report.pdf.

137   only the fighting in Libya: see "Per capita deaths in Arab uprisings," *The
        Mideastwire Blog*, May 12, 2011, mideastwire.wordpress.com/2011/05/12/
        per-capita-deaths-in-arab-uprisings.

138   Scholars have attributed: see for example "A History of Violence," by Steven
        Pinker, *The New Republic*, March 19, 2007, online at edge.org/3rd_culture/
        pinker07/pinker07_index.html; and "The Liberal Moment Fifteen
        Years On," by Nils Peter Gleditsch, *International Studies Quarterly*, vol.
        52, 2008, pp. 691-712. Both Pinker, a psychologist, and Gleditsch, a
        political scientist, suggest that global trade and communications might be
        contributing to the recent decline of war.

138   the media has helped: the novelist Kurt Vonnegut, some of whose
        writings are quite pessimistic about the prospects for world
        peace, nonetheless said in a 1982 speech that "thanks to modern
        communications, we now have something we never had before: reason to
        mourn deeply the death or wounding of any human being on any side in
        any war." See vonnegutweb.com/archives/arc_avoidingbigbang.html.

139   "the strongest non-trivial or non-tautological statement": I interviewed
        Bruce Russett at Yale on July 13, 2004, and by phone several times
        between 1991 and 2004. Unless indicated otherwise, quotations are
        from these interviews. Russett presents the case for democratic peace
        in *Hegemony and Democracy*, Routledge, 2001; and *Triangulating Peace*
        (co-written with John Oneal), Norton, 2001.

140   Freedom House categorizes: the Freedom House data are available on its
        website, freedomhouse.org/template.cfm?page=1.

140   Only 12 percent of humanity: *How War Began*, by Keith Otterbein, Texas
        A&M Press, 2004, p. 223-224.

141   "The reason why I'm so strong on democracy": Bush is quoted in "In the
        Name of Democracy," by Jonathan Power, the *New York Times*, February
        14, 2006, online at nytimes.com/2006/02/14/opinion/14iht-edpower.
        html. In 1968 the comedian and social activist Dick Gregory said: "When

we can make democracy work, we won't have to force it down peoples' throats. If it is really such a good idea, and if they can see it working, they'll steal it."

141 "emerging" democracies: the problems of new democracies are spelled out in *Electing to Fight*, by Edward Mansfield and Jack Snyder, MIT Press, 2005. In addition to this caveat, some critics claim that because "democracy" is difficult to define precisely, proponents can too easily categorize societies as democratic or un-democratic to support their theory. A column in *India Times*, January 31, 2006, online at atimes.com/atimes/Middle_East/ HA31Ak01.html, derides this sort of *post-hoc* definition as the "no true Scotsman" fallacy. You define a Scotsman according to some behavioral criterion, and when confronted with a Scotsman who behaves otherwise, you conclude that he is "no true Scotsman." Argument: "Ach! No Scotsman puts sugar on his porridge." Reply: "But my uncle Angus likes sugar with his porridge." Rebuttal: "Ah yes, but no *true* Scotsman puts sugar on his porridge."

141 I met Mueller: I spoke to Mueller at Ohio State on May 14 and 15, 2010. I have also communicated with him by phone and email before and since that date. My quotes of Mueller, unless otherwise indicated, are from the interview at Ohio State. Many of Mueller's writings can be found at his website, psweb.sbs.ohio-state.edu/faculty/jmueller.

142 "attitudes towards it have changed: "War Has Almost Ceased to Exist: An Assessment," by John Mueller, *Political Science Quarterly*, vol. 124, no. 2, 2009, p. 320.

142 "prolonged peace favors": *ibid.*, p. 301.

142 "almost always enlarges": *ibid.*, p. 301.

142 "All the great masterful races": I found this quote from Teddy Roosevelt in Zinn, *op. cit.*, p. 300.

142 War is "an institution": Mueller, *op. cit.*, p. 320.

143 "[W]e may be reaching a point": *ibid.*, p. 298.

144 Mueller discounts the view: see *Atomic Obsession*, by John Mueller, Oxford University Press, 2010.

144 "Even allowing for stupidity, ineptness": *ibid.*, p. 41.

145 home appliances and deer: see "Why Isn't There More Violence?" by John Mueller, *Security Studies*, vol. 13, no. 3, Spring 2004, p. 195; and "Hardly Existential: Thinking Rationally about Terrorism," by John Mueller and Mark Stewart, *Foreign Affairs*, April 2, 2010, online at foreignaffairs.com/articles/66186/john-mueller-and-mark-g-stewart/hardly-existential?page=3.

145 have killed six thousand Americans: the *Washington Post* maintains a tally of U.S. casualties in Iraq and Afghanistan at projects.washingtonpost.com/fallen.

145 "remnants of war": see Mueller's book *The Remnants of War*, Cornell University Press, 2004.

145 "predatory militia bands": Mueller, "War Has Almost Ceased to Exist," p. 321.

145 "cyber war": see "Cyber Combat: Act of War," by Siobhan Gorman and Julian Barnes, the *Wall Street Journal*, May 31, 2011.

146 "you don't have to get rid of weapons": Interview with Mueller, May 14, 2010.

147 war causes economic inequality: *The Real Price of War*, by Joshua Goldstein, New York University Press, 2004.

147 a self-described "pro-feminist": *War and Gender*, by Joshua Goldstein, Cambridge University Press, 2001, p. xiii.

147 limited their son's exposure: Goldstein told me about this parental strategy when I interviewed him at his home in Amherst, Massachusetts, on July 30, 2004.

147 "War is not a product of capitalism": Goldstein, *War and Gender*, p. 412.

147 "somewhat more pessimistic": *ibid.*, p. 412.

148 Costa Rica... was ranked number one: I found these data on Costa Rica's "happiness" in "The Happiest People," by Nicholas Kristof, the *New York Times*, January 6, 2010, online at nytimes.com/2010/01/07/opinion/07kristof.html.

148 "If you want peace, work for justice": this slogan has been attributed to both Pope Paul VI and H.L. Mencken.

Chapter Six: The Power of Nonviolence

151   I wrote up a few ideas: here are two other ideas I gave Centra: hiring
       volunteers to pretend to be members of terrorist "sleeper cells" to gain
       insight into terrorist thinking; and creating a website where anyone could
       anonymously submit plans for terrorist attacks.

152   "too political": the irony is that Sharp's first book, published in 1973,
       was funded by the Pentagon via the Defense Advanced Research Projects
       Agency.

152   "shy," "stoop-shouldered": "Shy U.S. Intellectual Created Playbook Used
       in a Revolution," by Sheryl Gay Stolberg, the *New York Times*, Feb. 6,
       2011, p. 1.

152   "helping to advance": "American Revolutionary," by Philip Shishkin, the
       Wall Street Journal, September 13, 2008.

153   bizarre animated video: The Iranian video can be found on YouTube,
       youtube.com/watch?v=6rGRY7p_sOo&feature=player_embedded.

153   his first major work: *The Politics of Nonviolent Action*, by Gene Sharp, Porter
       Sargent Publishers, 1973.

153   translated into more than thirty languages: Many of Sharp's writings
       can be downloaded from the website of the Albert Einstein Institution,
       aeinstein.org.

153   a wide variety of tactics: For a full list, see the appendix of *From
       Dictatorship to Democracy*, by Gene Sharp, The Albert Einstein Institution,
       1993.

154   "Do not the figures make it clear": Sharp, *The Politics of Nonviolent Action*,
       p. 30.

154   "consider it a shame to assist": *ibid.*, p. 32.

154   a low, gravelly growl: I interviewed Sharp at the Albert Einstein
       Institution in Boston on September 16, 2003.

156   "political power grows out of the barrel of a gun": *Webster's Quotationary*,
       edited by Leonard Roy Frank, Random House. 1999, p. 906.

156   working-class plebeians: Sharp, *The Politics of Nonviolent Action (op. cit.)*,
       pp. 75-76.

156   ordered Norwegian teachers: *ibid.*, p. 89.

157   "can end oppression": *A Force More Powerful*, by Peter Ackerman and Jack DuVall, Palgrave, 2000, p. 8.

157   Begin and Sadat shared the 1978 Nobel Peace Prize: see the Nobel Foundation write-up at nobelprize.org/nobel_prizes/peace/laureates/1978.

158   rape, robbery, and other crimes: For a balanced discussion of charges against U.N. workers, see "Is the UN Doomed?" by Tony Judt, the *New York Review of Books*, February 15, 2007, pp. 45-48.

158   "played a significant role": see the Nobel Foundation write-up at nobelprize.org/nobel_prizes/peace/laureates/1988/un.html.

158   A 2007 analysis by RAND: "A Comparative Evaluation of United Nations Peacekeeping," by James Dobbins, Rand Corporation, 2007, online at rand.org/pubs/testimonies/2007/RAND_CT284.pdf.

158   "It would be depressing": Gwynne Dyer, "The End of War," the *Toronto Star*, December 30, 2004, online at commondreams.org/views04/1230-05.htm.

159   one of his first acts... was to prohibit contras: see Arias's biography on the Nobel Foundation website, nobelprize.org/nobel_prizes/peace/laureates/1987/arias-bio.html.

160   "Apocalyptic prophets abound": You can find Arias's lecture at nobelprize.org/nobel_prizes/peace/laureates/1987/arias-lecture.html.

161   was keen on holy wars: *Sex and War*, by Malcolm Potts and Thomas Hayden, Benbella, 2008, p. 244.

161   should be waged ruthlessly: *Just and Unjust Wars*, by Michael Walzer, Basic Books, 2000 (first published 1977), p. 47. This book by Walzer, a social scientist, provides a good introduction to Just War theory. The book is marred, however, by Walzer's condescending dismissal of nonviolent resistance and his rejection of a world without war as a utopian dream, p. 329: "In our myths and visions, the end of war is also the end of secular history. Those of us trapped within that history, who see no end to it, have no choice but to fight on, defending the values to which we are committed, unless or until some alternative means of defense can be found."

162   Bombs dropped by NATO planes: see "Libyan Rebels' Convoy Mistakenly

Hit by NATO, Rebel General Says," by C.J. Chivers and Kareem Fahim, the *New York Times*, April 8, 2011, p. A12; "Libya: Nato admits civilian deaths in Tripoli air raid," by Nick Hopkins, the *Guardian*, June 20, 2011, and "Libyan rebels accused of reprisal attacks," the *Washington Post*, by Sudarsan Raghavan, May 21, 2011.

162   In a 2003 essay: "Power of Love," by Alastair McIntosh, *Resurgence*, no. 219, July/August 2003, pp. 42-44.

163   "The non-violent resistors will have won the day": this Gandhi quote is from *Is There No Other Way?* by Michael Nagler, Berkeley Hills Book, 2001, p. 249.

164   "does not make wars less likely": I found the Einstein quotes in this section in an essay, "Einstein and War Resistance," on the website of the International Peace Bureau, ipb.org/einstein.html.

164   Zinn flew in a bombing raid: Zinn tells this story in his memoir *You Can't Be Neutral on a Moving Train*, Beacon Press, 2002 (originally published 1994).

164   when I interviewed him: I interviewed Zinn at his home in Massachusetts on September 17, 2003.

165   "I see this as the central issue of our time": Zinn, *op. cit.*, p. 101.

166   In an episode of *60 Minutes*: John Mueller describes this episode in *Atomic Obsessions*, Oxford University Press, 2010. pp. 134-135.

167   "just policing": Gerald Schlabach gives an overview of just policing in "Just Policing, Not War," *America: The National Catholic Weekly*, July 7, 2003, online at americamagazine.org/content/article.cfm?article_id=3051.

168   drone attacks: the U.S. military has deployed more than 7,000 unmanned airborne vehicles, or drones, according to the security analyst P.W. Singer of the Brookings Institution. At least forty-three nations—including England, Israel, and Iran—have already deployed or are building drones and other military robots, he says. The Obama administration has carried out far more drone attacks than the Bush administration. The number of attacks in Pakistan alone in 2010 was 117, more than all previous years combined, according to "Americans Launch Drone Missile Attacks Despite Recent Pakistani Objections," by Eric Schmitt, the *New York Times*, April 13, 2011. A 2010 United Nations report, online at www2.ohchr.org/english/

bodies/hrcouncil/docs/14session/A.HRC.14.24.Add6.pdf, complains that
drone attacks—especially in Pakistan and Yemen, nations with which the
United States is not at war—are "doing grave damage to the rules designed
to protect the right to life and prevent extrajudicial executions." A 2009
Brookings Institution report, online at brookings.edu/opinions/2009/0714_
targeted_killings_byman.aspx?p=1, estimates that U.S. drone attacks in
Pakistan kill ten civilians on average for every militant.

168   We sell weapons to other nations, and to their adversaries: The Stockholm
        International Peace Research Institute, SIPRI, sipri.org/, documents how
        the U.S., by far the world's biggest arms dealer, supplies arms for races
        in many volatile regions. The U.S. sells fighter jets and other advanced
        weaponry to both Pakistan and its arch–enemy India, and to Israel and its
        unfriendly Arab neighbors. In the fall of 2010, the Obama administration
        announced a $60 billion sale of fighters and other weapons to Saudi Arabia,
        the largest such sale in history. U.S. officials issued reassurances that the U.S.
        would help Israel maintain its superiority over Saudi Arabia and all other
        potentially hostile states in the region. See "Pentagon plans $60 billion
        arms sale to Saudi Arabia," by Dana Hedgpeth, the *Washington Post*, October
        21, 2010.

169   most nations have already done: see Amnesty International's list of nations
        that have abolished the death penalty at amnesty.org/en/death-penalty/
        abolitionist-and-retentionist-countries.

169   Paul Chappell... two essays: *Will War Ever End?* Rvive Books, 2009, and
        The End of War, Easton Studio Press, 2010.

171   "kill each other out of our self-righteousness": "Francis Collins: The
        Scientist as Believer," by John Horgan, *National Geographic*, February
        2007, online at ngm.nationalgeographic.com/ngm/0702/voices.html.

172   Wilson asks Christians to join him: *The Creation*, W.W. Norton, 2006.

172   "dangerous, defeatist belief": John F. Kennedy's "peace speech" can be found
        online at jfklibrary.org/Research/Ready-Reference/JFK-Speeches.aspx.

173   "not only human, but protohuman": *Rising Up and Rising Down*, by
        William Vollmann, Harper Perennial, 2004, p. 23. (This is the abridged
        edition of the original, seven-volume edition published by McSweeney's.)

173   "human violence itself cannot be altered": *ibid.*, p. 25.

173   "putting aside any notion": *ibid.*, p. 21.

174   "No one knows enough": I found this quote in Nagler, *op. cit.*, p. 272.

Epilogue: In Defense of Free Will

175   "It is hard to imagine": *The Grand Design*, by Stephen Hawking and
       Leonard Mlodinow, Bantam Books, 2010, p. 32.

176   "the moon were gifted": I found this Einstein quote in *The Illusion of
       Conscious Will*, by Daniel Wegner, Bradford Books, 2002, p. 342.

176   "What you're aware of is a decision": I interviewed Francis Crick in
       November 1991 and wrote about his views on free will in my 1996
       book *The End of Science*, Broadway Books, 1996. The man with whom
       Crick co-discovered the double helix, James Watson, was a much
       more egregious biological determinist, as indicated by "Fury at DNA
       pioneer's theory: Africans Are Less Intelligent than Westerners,"
       by Cahal Milmo, the *Independent*, October 17, 2007, online at
       independent.co.uk/news/science/fury-at-dna-pioneers-theory-africans-
       are-less-intelligent-than-westerners-394898.html. Watson confesses
       to being "inherently gloomy about the prospect of Africa" because
       "all our social policies are based on the fact that their intelligence is
       the same as ours—whereas all the testing says not really." Watson
       is essentially blaming Africa's problems on the innate inferiority
       of blacks. For an overview of research showing that environmental
       factors—including poor schools and parenting—explain poor black
       performance on IQ tests and other measures of intelligence far better
       than genetic theories do, see *Intelligence and How to Get It*, by Richard
       Nisbet, W.W. Norton, 2009.

176   "Our belief in free will": *The Moral Landscape*, by Sam Harris, Free Press,
       2010, p. 141.

177   "So it turns out": "How Free Is Your Will?" by Daniela Schiller
       and David Carmel, *Scientific American*, March 22, 2011, online at
       scientificamerican.com/article.cfm?id=how-free-is-your-will&WT.
       mc_id=SA_DD_20110322.

178   "confabulations": Wegner, *op. cit.*, p. 171.

178   "not what tradition declares it to be": *Freedom Evolves*, by Daniel Dennett, Viking, 2003, p. 13.

179   "an evolved creation of human activity": *ibid.*, p. 13.

179   "point to a significant value": "The Value of Believing in Free Will," by Kathleen Vohs and Jonathan Schooler, *Psychological Science*, vol. 19, no. 1, 2008, pp. 49-54, online at csom.umn.edu/assets/91974.pdf.

SELECTED BIBLIOGRAPHY

Below is an annotated list of books (and two documentaries) that I found especially helpful for understanding war and related activities, even if I disagree with some of their assertions therein.

Ackerman Peter, and DuVall, Jack, *A Force More Powerful*, Palgrave, 2000. Ackerman, a political scientist, and DuVall, a veteran broadcast journalist, wrote this book to complement their documentary television series, also called *A Force More Powerful*, which highlights the major successes of nonviolent activism in the twentieth century.

Baker, Nicholson, *Human Smoke*, Simon & Schuster, 2008. As strikingly original a writer of nonfiction as fiction, Baker assembles a collage of historical documents from the run-up to World War II that raises questions about the morality and inevitability of the ultimate Just War.

Bourke, Joanna, *An Intimate History of Killing*, Basic Books, 1999. In this compilation of anecdotes from the First and Second World Wars and the Vietnam War, the British historian Bourke exposes the ferocity that combat can unleash in men and women.

Chagnon, Napoleon A., *Yanomamö: The Fierce People*, Holt, Rinehart and Winston, 1968. One of the best selling ethnographic works ever, Chagnon's gripping study of tribal people living deep in the Amazon is often cited as evidence that males are born warriors, though Chagnon himself never makes that claim.

Chagnon, Napoleon A., *Yanomamö: The Last Days of Eden*, Harcourt Brace Jovanovich, 1992. In this somewhat melancholy follow-up book, Chagnon provides a more rounded portrayal of the Yanomamö and mourns the destruction of their lands and culture by the relentless encroachment of "civilization."

De Waal, Frans, *The Age of Empathy*, Three Rivers Press, 2009. Highlighting the positive personality traits of chimpanzees and other primates, de Waal, a leading primatologist, rebuts the popular, pessimistic meme that we are "killer apes" doomed to endless violence.

Diamond, Jared, *Collapse*, Viking Penguin, 2005. Societies that over-consume their resources and over-invest in militarism often collapse into violent chaos, the polymath Diamond warns, but we still have time, he says, to take steps to avert catastrophe.

Ehrenreich, Barbara, *Blood Rites*, Metropolitan Books, 1997. The progressive journalist Ehrenreich, who studied biology in college, depicts war as a lethal, mutable meme. She also argues, less persuasively, that war stems not from our ancestors' innate aggression but from their fear of predators.

Fry, Douglas P., *The Human Potential for Peace*, Oxford University Press, 2006. The anthropologist Fry mounts a persuasive critique—based on a close examination of research in anthropology and archaeology—of the claim that war is deeply rooted in human nature and prehistory.

Goldstein, Joshua S., *War and Gender*, Cambridge University Press, 2001. A political scientist, Goldstein provides an exhaustive exploration of how females as well as males have contributed to the perpetuation of war, which has in turn shaped cultural concepts of masculinity and femininity.

Grossman, Dave, *On Killing*, Little, Brown, 1996. Even more surprising than this book's central theme—that most soldiers are reluctant to kill—is that its author is a former Ranger, West Point professor, and lieutenant colonel in the Army.

Hedges, Chris, *War Is a Force That Gives Us Meaning*, Anchor Books, 2002. A former war correspondent eloquently describes war as a deadly addiction but seems to project his own fascination with armed conflict onto the rest of us.

Hrdy, Sarah Blaffer, *Mothers and Others*, Belknap Press, 2009. One of the world's leading anthropologists argues that familial relations played a larger role than warfare in shaping our ancestors' psyches.

Junger, Sebastian, *War*, Twelve, 2010. Junger provides a gripping description of his experience as a journalist living in Restrepo, an outpost of American soldiers in one of Afghanistan's most violent regions.

Junger, Sebastian, and Hetherington, Tim, *Restrepo*, 2010. Made by Junger and the photographer Tim Hetherington (killed in Libya in 2011), this documentary provides an almost unbearably intense immersion into the lives of young American combat soldiers.

Keegan, John, *A History of Warfare*, Alfred A. Knopf, 1993. One of the world's foremost historians of war provides an Olympian narrative of warfare from prehistory up through the end of the cold war. Keegan ends with a hopeful vision of the end of war—but not the end of warriors.

Keeley, Lawrence H., *War Before Civilization*, Oxford University Press, 1996. Together with *Demonic Males* and *Constant Battles* (listed below), this book has helped propagate the idea that war is ancient and innate, even though it provides abundant contrary data.

LeBlanc, Steven A., with Register, Katherine E., *Constant Battles*, St. Martin's Press, 2003. The Harvard archaeologist accepts the thesis of his colleague Richard Wrangham that war is ancient and innate while claiming that most wars stem from overpopulation and resource scarcity.

Mead, Margaret, *Coming of Age in Samoa*, William Morrow and Company, 1928. Mead's best-selling first book, like all her subsequent work, contends that we have many more options than biologically oriented theorists of human nature would have us believe.

Morris, Earle, *The Fog of War* (documentary film), 2003. This extended, annotated interview with Robert McNamara—a cold war technocrat who played a role in the firebombing of Japan during World War II, the Cuban Missile Crisis, and the escalation of the Vietnam War—reveals how militarism can transform an extremely intelligent, decent man into a self-described war criminal.

Mukerjee, Madhusree, *Churchill's Secret War*, Basic Books, 2010. Madhusree, a physicist-turned-journalist from a prominent Indian family, presents evidence that one of World War II's heroes was also a racist, whose cruel policies toward Indians caused a famine that killed millions in the early 1940s.

Mueller, John, *Quiet Cataclysm*, HarperCollins, 1995. In this book and others (*The Remnants of War, Atomic Obsession, Overblown*), Mueller, a political scientist, makes the case that humanity may finally be ready to abandon war, but first we have to stop overreacting to threats real and imagined.

Otterbein, Keith F., *How War Began*, Texas A&M University Press, 2004. An anthropologist, Otterbein suspects that our ancestors may have engaged in group conflict as early as 2 million years ago when they began hunting big game. Notwithstanding this unsubstantiated hypothesis, Otterbein's book is full of data and conjectures on violence in prehistory.

Potts, Malcolm, and Hayden, Thomas, *Sex and War*, BenBella Books, 2008. This book by Potts, a physician and women's-rights activist, and Hayden, a journalist, relies too much on the war-is-ancient-and-innate idea, but redeems itself by providing a wealth of information on correlates of conflict, and especially the link between female empowerment and peace.

Richardson, Lewis Fry, *Statistics of Deadly Quarrels*, edited by Quincy Wright and Carl C. Lienau, Boxwood Press, 1960. A Quaker pacifist and physicist whose mathematical models of weather in the 1920s laid the foundation for modern forecasting, Richardson spent the last three decades of his life analyzing armed conflict. This eccentric but still relevant classic of war studies, edited and published after Richardson's death in 1953, was the result.

Russett, Bruce, and Oneal, John, *Triangulating Peace*, Norton, 2001. In this excellent introduction to democratic-peace theory, two political scientists argue that democracy—plus trade and international institutions that promote understanding—are helping make the world more peaceful.

Sachs, Jeffrey D., *Common Wealth*, Penguin, 2008. In this follow-up to his best seller *The End of Poverty*, the renowned economist lays out a plan for ending extreme poverty while preserving the environment. As a bonus, Sachs suggests, the world would also become much less violent.

Sapolsky, Robert M., *The Trouble with Testosterone*, Touchstone, 1997. An expert on neuroscience, genetics, and primatology, among other biological fields, Sapolsky entertainingly skewers reductionist models of violence and other behaviors.

Sharp, Gene, *The Politics of Nonviolent Action*, P. Sargent Publisher, 1973. This is the first of a series of books in which Sharp, a political scientist, argues that nonviolent action can be much more effective than violence at ending injustice and tyranny and bringing about political change.

Singer, P.W., *Wired for War*, Penguin, 2009. A defense analyst, Singer provides an alarming report on the U.S. military's increasing reliance on high-tech weapons, including ground-based robots and drones such as the Predator, which allows operators in California to kill people in Pakistan.

Sledge, Eugene B., *With the Old Breed*, Presidio Press, 1981. This gritty, plainspoken memoir by Sledge, a Marine who fought in the bloody battles in the Pacific between the U.S. and Japan during World War II, should be required reading for anyone who doubts that war is hell.

Stockholm International Peace Research Institute Yearbook. Published annually by one of the world's foremost defense think tanks, this is an excellent source on trends in armed conflicts, arms, armies, and defense spending. The statistic that stands out for me: the U.S. spends almost as much on defense as all other nations combined.

Vollmann, William T., *Rising Up and Rising Down*, Ecco, 2004. In this abridged edition of a seven-volume work originally published by McSweeney's, the idiosyncratic novelist and journalist Vollmann ponders the varieties of human violence and tries to derive a "calculus" for determining when violence is justified.

Walzer, Michael, *Just and Unjust Wars*, Basic Books, 1977. A political philosopher, Walzer examines World War II, the Vietnam War, and other conflicts through the lens of Just War theory, which seeks to distinguish good wars from bad ones. Like Vollmann, Walzer suggests that we will never achieve a world without war, and so the best we can do is to minimize their harm.

Wrangham, Richard, and Peterson, Dale, *Demonic Males*, Houghton Mifflin, 1996. This book by the anthropologist Wrangham and journalist Peterson revived the old "killer ape" meme in spite of a lack of solid evidence.

Zimbardo, Philip, *The Lucifer Effect*, Random House, 2007. Zimbardo describes the famous Stanford Prison Experiment and teases out its implications, the most important of which is that atrocities usually stem from bad barrels, or situations, rather than bad apples, people with cruel dispositions.

Zinn, Howard, *A People's History of the United States*, HarperCollins, 1999 (fourth edition). The historian and political activist documents the dark side of American history, beginning with the extraordinarily cruel treatment by Columbus of natives he encountered in the New World.

Zinn, Howard, *You Can't Be Neutral on a Moving Train*, Beacon Press, 1994. In this memoir, Zinn recalls his participation in a bombing mission that probably killed civilians in France during World War II. His discovery of this fact made Zinn realize that even supposedly moral wars inevitably have immoral consequences.

ACKNOWLEDGEMENTS

I've been talking about war for almost as long as I can remember with almost everyone I know, including family, friends, taxi drivers, and random people I meet at parties. I'd like to thank certain people who encouraged me to pursue this project and helped me formulate my thoughts (which is not to say that they will agree with everything in this book). They include my students and colleagues at Stevens Institute of Technology, and especially Jim McClellan, Harold Dorn, Garry Dobbins, and Lisa Dolling; my fellow science journalists David Berreby, George Johnson, Robin Lloyd, Madhusree Mukerjee, Phil Ross, Gary Stix, Karen Wright, Robert Wright, and Glenn Zorpette; and my buddies Chris Bremser, Robert Hutchinson, Jim O'Rourke, David Rothenberg, Tyler Volk, and David Zindell. Scientists and scholars who were especially helpful include Robert Carneiro, Napoleon Chagnon, Frans de Waal, Carol and Melvin Ember, Brian Ferguson, Randall Forsberg, Douglas Fry, Joshua Goldstein, Jonathan Haas, Thomas Homer-Dixon, Sarah Blaffer Hrdy, Melvin Konner, Steven LeBlanc, John Mueller, Keith Otterbein, Steven Pinker, Rudolph Rummel, Bruce Russett, Jeffrey Sachs, Kirkpatrick Sale, Robert Sapolsky, Gene Sharp, J. David Singer, Peter W. Singer, Robert Sussman, Erik Trinkaus, Edward Wilson, Richard Wrangham, Duane Friesen, Jim Juhnke, Julie Hart, Stan Eitzen, Patty Shelly, Paul Lewis, Wayne Wiens, Mark Jantzen, Brian Turner, Kirsten Zerger, Philip Zimbardo, and Howard Zinn.

I'll always be grateful to Dave Eggers and everyone at McSweeney's, and especially to Jesse Nathan—the toughest, hardest working, and best editor I've ever had—for believing in this book. Thanks also to Victoria Havlicek, Jordan Karnes, Jill Haberkern, Amanda Foushee, Charlotte Locke, Jennifer Florin, and Libby Wachtler for reading, proofing, fact checking, and otherwise helping to develop this book. I'm thankful most of all to Valerie Cates, whose faith in me—if not in the rest of humanity—gave me the strength to finish this book.

ABOUT THE AUTHOR

John Horgan teaches and directs the Center for Science
Writings at Stevens Institute of Technology, Hoboken,
New Jersey. He writes regularly for *Scientific American*,
the *Chronicle of Higher Education*, and *BBC Knowledge
Magazine*, among other publications. He is also a science
correspondent for Bloggingheads.tv, an internet chat show.
His previous books include *The End of Science* (Addison
Wesley, 1996), *The Undiscovered Mind* (Free Press, 1999),
and *Rational Mysticism* (Houghton Mifflin, 2003). He
lives in New York's Hudson Valley.